Trustees and Officers
of
Indiana University
1950 to 1982

Trustees and Officers of Indiana University 1950 to 1982

ELEANOR L. ROEHR
Special Assistant to the President

Indiana University
Bloomington

Copyright © 1983 by Indiana University
All rights reserved
No part of this book may be reproduced or utilized in any form or by any means, electronic or mechanical, including photocopying and recording, or by any information storage and retrieval system, without permission in writing from the publisher.

Manufactured in the United States of America

Library of Congress Cataloging in Publication Data

Indiana University.
Trustees and officers of Indiana University, 1950 to 1982.
1. Indiana University. 2. College administrators—Indiana—Biography. 3. College trustees—Indiana—Biography. I. Roehr, Eleanor L. II. Title.
LD2515.I52   1983   378.772'255   83-47510
ISBN 0-253-36095-1
1 2 3 4 5 87 86 85 84 83

Contents

List of Illustrations	vii
Preface	xi
Trustees	1
Presidents	119
After each President a chronology of important events by campus	
Vice-Presidents	157
Chancellors	211
Secretaries and Treasurers	253
Board of Trustees' Yearly Pictures	267
Index	301

Illustrations

Trustees

Allen, Frank Emerson	1940–53, 1954–55	2
Bannon, William Gregory	1971–	5
Black, Joseph Morton	1972–	8
Campbell, Alexander Morton	1948–53	10
Danielson, Donald Carroll	1959–80	13
Davis, Merrill Stamper	1950–53, 1959–62	16
Early, John Ehret	1965–71	19
Eschbach, Jesse Ernest II	1965–70	22
Feltus, Paul Lambert	1934–47, 1949–57	24
Gates, Robert Edwards	1969–	26
Geiger, Dillon Donald	1947–50, 1953–54, 1956–59	29
Gonso, Harry Lee	1976–	32
Gray, Carl M.	1967–75	34
Gray, James Walter*	1981–83	37
Gutman, Carolyn Prickett	1974–	39
Hastings, John Simpson	1936–59	42
Helmke, Walter Edward	1954–56	45
Henley, George Washington	1945–51	48
Hickam, Willis	1953–65	52
Hillis, Glen Raymond	1953–54	54
Inskeep, Harriett Simmons	1962–71	57
Lash, Donald Ray	1970–72	60
Long, Clarence William	1975–	62
Lucas, Robert Anthony	1967–70	64
McCarty, Charles Walter	1945–62	67
McCrea, Robert Franklin	1959–65	70

* Student Trustee

McKinney, Frank Edward, Sr.	1962–69	72
McKinney, Frank Edward, Jr.	1973–76	76
Maurer, Mary Rieman	1945–63	79
Menke, Robert Henry	1966–72	81
Miller, Jeanne Seidel	1971–74	84
Mohr, William Hall*	1979–81	86
Polley, Elizabeth Blumberg	1980–	89
Pulse, Earl Burton	1955–59	92
Riley, John Stewart	1957–63	94
Rogers, Donald Aquilla	1963–66	98
Shively, Leslie Curtis*	1976–77	101
Stoner, Richard Burkett	1972–	103
Thomas, Ray Cecil	1952–67	106
Widaman, John Daniel II	1970–72	109
Wilcox, Howard Samuel	1963–66	111
Wildermuth, Ora Leonard	1925–52	114
Wolfe, James Willard*	1977–79	117

Presidents

Wells, Herman B	1937–62, Sept.–Nov. 1968	120
Stahr, Elvis Jacob, Jr.	1962–68	128
Sutton, Joseph Lee	1968–71	136
Ryan, John William	1971–	142

Vice-Presidents

Ashton, John William	1952–65	158
Bonus, Thaddeus M.	1976–80	162
Braden, Samuel Edward	1959–67	164
Briscoe, Herman Thompson	1942–59	167
Carter, Byrum Earl, Jr.	1974–75	170
Collins, Ralph Leonard	1959–63	172
Derge, David Richard, Jr.	1968–72	175
Franklin, Joseph Amos	1948–71	178
Gros Louis, Kenneth R. R.	1980–	181
Hartley, Joseph Robert	1968–72	184
Heffner, Ray Lorenzo, Jr.	1964–66	187

* Student Trustee

Irwin, Glenn Ward, Jr.#	1973–	190
Liebenow, J. Gus	1972–74	192
Merritt, Lynne Lionel, Jr.	1965–75	195
O'Neil, Robert M.	1975–80	198
Pinnell, William George	1974–	200
Ryan, John William (see Presidents)	1968–70	
Snyder, John William	1967–69	204
Sutton, Joseph Lee (see Presidents)	1966–68	
Williams, Edgar Gene	1973–	206
Wright, Wendell William	1952–59	209

\# IUPUI Campus at Indianapolis

Chancellors

Bogle, Victor Morton, Kokomo	1969–79	212
Bowman, Sylvia Edmonia, Regional Campuses	1972–75	215
Broyles, Ralph Edward, Fort Wayne #	1969–74	218
Carter, Byrum Earl, Jr., Bloomington (see Vice-Presidents)	1969–74	
Crooks, Edwin William, New Albany	1969–	220
Guisti, Joseph Paul, Fort Wayne #	1979–	223
Goerke, Glenn Allan, Richmond	1981–	226
Grohsmeyer, Frederick Andrew, Jr.,* Richmond	1973–76	229
Hine, Maynard Kiplinger,# Indianapolis	1968–73	232
McNeill, Robert Joseph, Gary	1970–74	235
Orescanin, Danilo, Gary	1975–	238
Penrod, Kenneth Earl,† Indianapolis	1965–69	241
Ryan, John William, Regional Campuses (see Presidents)	1969–70	
Schilt, Alexander F., Richmond	1976–80	244
Schwartz, Donald, Fort Wayne #	1974–78	246
Thompson, Hugh Lee, Kokomo	1980–	248

* Actual title was Director; he pre-dated the Chancellor system.

\# Joint operation with Purdue University on these campuses.

† Actual title was Provost for the Medical Center in Indianapolis. This position was abolished, and in the process of reorganization. A Vice-Presidency was created for the IUPU Campus in Indianapolis.

Wells, Herman B, University   1962–
  (see Presidents)
Wolfson, Lester Marvin, South Bend   1969–   251

Secretaries

Cookson, Thomas Aubrey   1936–37, 1942–51   254
Reed, Fenwick Thomas   1951–66   257
Harrell, Charles Edwin   1967–81   259
Burton, Robert Ermer   1981–   262

Treasurers

Cookson, Thomas Aubrey   1937–42
  (see Secretaries)
Franklin, Joseph Amos   1946–71
  (see Vice-Presidents)
Pinnell, William George   1971–74
  (see Vice-Presidents)
Mulholland, John D.   1974–   265

Board of Trustees

Chart of Trustees' Tenure   268
Yearly Pictures, 1949–50 to 1981–82   269–300

Preface

This volume continues the biographical material through 1982 of the Officers and Trustees of Indiana University, first published in 1951 under the authorship of Dr. Burton Dorr Myers as *Trustees and Officers of Indiana University, 1820 to 1950*. Biographical research was drawn from materials in the Indiana University Archives, the Trustees' Office, and other published sources. All biographical materials were checked by the subject if living, and with a close relative if the subject was deceased. Subjects from Dr. Myers's book who were still in office or who had died since the earlier book was published have had their biographies updated with this volume.

The degrees appearing in parentheses after a name refer to Indiana University degrees, unless specifically stated otherwise.

The author is indebted to the University Archives, particularly to Dr. Daniel Rubey, for the early in-depth biographic research; to Claude Rich for both data and clues to sources of data from his vast knowledge of Indiana lore; and to Dorothy Collins for her assistance in selecting the useful and pertinent data pertaining to that portion of Dr. Herman B Wells's tenure not included in the previous volume.

Trustees and Officers of Indiana University 1950 to 1982

Trustees

Frank Emerson Allen

Frank Emerson Allen, 1891–1981

TRUSTEE, 1940–1953, 1954–1955

Frank Emerson Allen, of St. Joseph County, superintendent of schools, South Bend, Indiana, was born in Summitville, Madison County, Indiana, March 11, 1891, the son of Joseph A. and Jane (Sheek) Allen. The family, of Scotch-Irish descent, emigrated from England, settled in South Carolina, and about 1845 came to Indiana. Frank's father was a farmer and later became a merchant in Summitville.

Frank attended grade and high school in Summitville until 1908. For the next two years, he was a student in Losantville, a Randolph County consolidated high school, from which he was graduated in 1910. During the next four years he taught in a township school in Randolph County and spent his summers as a student at Indiana University. From June, 1914, to June, 1916, he was in continuous residence at Indiana University, where he was active in school affairs. He played baseball as a freshman, was a member of the football team for three years, and won a letter in basketball. He was graduated with the A.B. degree in June, 1916, and received the A. M. degree in 1924.

In 1916–1917 Mr. Allen was Principal of the Losantville school during the first semester, and during the second semester taught mathematics in the Mount Vernon High School. For the next two years he was head of the Department of Mathematics and coach of athletics in the New Castle High School. From 1919 to 1921 he was principal and and coach in the same high school. In 1921 he became Principal of Central High School, Muncie, and in 1925 he was elected Superintendent of the Schools of Muncie, where he remained until 1931, when he was elected Superintendent of Schools of South Bend.

On March 13, 1920, Mr. Allen married Helen A. Dykes, of Middletown, Indiana, who died December 10, 1943. On December 25, 1944, he married Kathleen Moore, of Muncie, Indiana.

Mr. Allen was a Knight Templar, a thirty-second-degree Scottish Rite Mason, and a Shriner. He was a life member of the National Education Association, a member of the Indiana University Alumni Council, and served as a member of the Indiana State Board of Education (1931-1936). He was a President and Director of Northern Indiana Society for Crippled Children and of the Indiana Town and City Superintendents Association. He organized the South Bend chapter of Phi Delta Kappa, national educational honor fraternity.

In 1940 he was elected by the State Board of Education as a Trustee of Indiana University to fill the unexpired term of Val F. Nolan, and served consecutive terms until 1953 when he was replaced by Glenn R. Hillis. Hillis, however, served for only a year, resigning for health reasons in 1954, at which time Allen was reappointed. In March of the following year, Allen was appointed Indiana University Athletic Director and Professor of Education, officially assuming these positions on June 15, 1955. He continued to serve on the Board of Trustees at Governor Craig's pleasure until September 10, 1955 when he was replaced by Earl B. Pulse.

Frank was an ambitious and energetic Athletic Director. He was responsible for the construction of the New Fieldhouse, the 43,344-seat football stadium, new football practice fields, an 18-hole golf course, a 9-hole par 3 course, and a driving range.

In recognition of his many accomplishments in the Athletics Department, the Indiana University Chapter of Sigma Delta Chi, professional journalism society, honored Allen with the Leather Medal in 1961.

Allen retired from Indiana University in June, 1961. He died in Muncie, Indiana, on November 18, 1981.

William Gregory Bannon, 1921–
Trustee, 1971–

William Gregory Bannon, physician and abiding supporter of Indiana University athletics, son of Freeman R. and Nell (Gregory) Bannon, was born in Kokomo, Indiana, on December 18, 1921. His father received his medical degree from In-

William Gregory Bannon

diana University in 1911. William was graduated from Kokomo High School in 1939 and entered Indiana University, where he obtained his bachelor's degree (1943) and his M.D. (1945). He later took an M.S. in medicine at the University of Minnesota (1952), after having served in the U.S. Army from 1943 to 1948.

On July 4, 1942, William married Jane Alexander, who obtained an A.B. from Indiana University (1943). They had three children, all of whom were graduated from Indiana University: Sue Bannon Latham (A.B. 1966), Pamela Bannon Denning (B.S. 1970), and Lynn Ellen Bannon Crawford (A.B. 1975).

Dr. Bannon is a member of Phi Kappa Psi, Rotary, Elks, the Presbyterian Church, and a life member of the Alumni Association, which he has served as a member of its Executive Council. He also has found time to serve the community as President of the United Fund for Terre Haute, Vice-President of the Terre Haute Chamber of Commerce and of the Terre Haute Council of Churches. He is a Director of the Fort Harrison Savings and Loan Association of Terre Haute and of the Valley Federal Savings and Loan.

His medically-related activities have included directorships on the State Cancer Board, State Mental Health Association, State Maternal Mortality Commission, and State Regional Health Planning Commission for Nursing Education; membership on the Mayor's Commission on Human Relations, American Board of Internal Medicine, and the American College of Physicians; and a term as President of the Medical Alumni Association. He is an Assistant Professor of Medicine at the IU School of Medicine. Dr. Bannon was named "Physician of the Year" by the Indiana Mental Health Association in 1968. The monetary award that accompanied this honor was turned over to the Indiana University Scholarship Fund.

William Bannon long has had an intense interest in sports, particularly as related to Indiana University, and even before becoming a Trustee he often voiced his interests on athletic matters to the University administration. He has been a recruiter of athletes for Indiana University and has served as President of the Vigo County Varsity Club. He is a member of the Varsity Club's Hoosier 100. Bannon was first appointed to the Indiana University Board of Trustees in 1971 and reappointed in 1974, 1977, and 1980.

Joseph Morton Black, 1918–
TRUSTEE, 1972–

Joseph Morton Black, physician, son of Morton Colfax and Mae (Baker) Black, was born in Seymour, Indiana, on September 17, 1918. He graduated from Seymour High School in 1937 and entered Indiana University, where he obtained his A.B. (1941) and his M.D. (1944). He served his internship and residency at Indianapolis General Hospital (1944 to 1946) and, upon completion, entered the United States Army Medical Corps. Dr. Black served in the Army from 1946 to 1948 and has been a practicing physician in Seymour ever since.

On December 27, 1942, he married Mary A. Elsner, whose father, Edward Peter Elsner, received an LL.B. in 1904 from Indiana University. Mary's mother, Mae MacDonald, and her grandfather also attended Indiana University. The Blacks had three children, all of whom attended Indiana University: Deborah Ann (B.S. 1969), Susan Annette Black Edwards (B.S. 1970) and Joseph M. Black, Jr. (B.S. 1977, J.D. 1981). Mary Elsner Black died in June 1969, and Dr. Black married Jane L. Thompson on February 7, 1971.

At Indiana University, Joseph participated in freshman football and basketball, was senior baseball manager, was a member of Sigma Alpha Epsilon (which bestowed upon him the Order of the Phoenix), Blue Key, the Sphinx Club, Nu Sigma Nu medical fraternity, and the "I" Men's Association. The latter organization presented Dr. Black with the coveted Zora G. Clevenger Award in November 1978, and in 1980 he was made a Distinguished Alumnus of the Medical School.

Dr. Black has been active in the medical field outside of his personal practice as a Jackson County Health Officer since 1962. He was the originator and stimulus of the Indiana State Medical Education Plan, a President of the Indiana State Medical Association (and recipient of its outstanding service

Joseph Morton Black

award), a member and Vice-Chairman of the Board of Governors of the Riley Memorial Association, founder and Treasurer of the Indiana Medical Political Action Committee, and Chairman of the Indiana Blue Shield Board (1970–   ).

In addition to his medical interests Dr. Black has been active in the Seymour Community School Holding Corporation, having served as a Director and Vice-President of that organization. He is a board member of the Seymour Boys Club (and a past President of the Board), a life member and past President of the IU Alumni Association (1965–66), a past officer and Director of the Seymour Chamber of Commerce, and a Director of the Jackson County Bank.

Dr. Black was first elected to the Board of Trustees in 1972 and has been re-elected thrice to consecutive terms. He is a Democrat and has been active in the Methodist Church, Rotary, Masons, Elks, Eagles, and American Legion. He also is a member of the Columbia Club in Indianapolis, the Varsity Club's Hoosier Hundred, the IU Foundation's Pacesetter Club and its Well House Society.

Alexander Morton Campbell, 1907–1968
Trustee, 1948–1953

Alexander Morton Campbell, United States Attorney, Assistant Attorney-General of the United States, was born at Coldwater, Ohio, April 14, 1907, the son of Samuel T. and Elsie (Bolman) Campbell. Alexander was descended from Scotch Presbyterians who lived in Glasgow prior to their migration to America. Alexander's father was born in Virginia. His father died in 1919, and in 1920 his mother moved to Fort Wayne, where Alexander attended grade and high school. After high school he entered Olivet College, Michigan, where he spent two years (1925–1927) taking a pre-law course. In the fall of 1927 he became a student at the Indiana University School of Law and was graduated in 1930 with the degree LL.B.

During his three years at Indiana University Alexander was active in campus affairs. He was president of the senior law class, of his social fraternity, Delta Chi, of the student

Alexander Morton Campbell

Y.M.C.A., and of the young people's group of the Christian Church. He was a member of the Board of Aeons, the Interfraternity Council, the Tau Kappa Alpha debating and forensic fraternity, and the Theta Phi law fraternity. He was awarded the Niezer debating trophy in 1929 and the National Keystone Award of the Boys' Clubs of America.

He was admitted to the Indiana bar in 1929 and began to practice law at Fort Wayne, in June, 1930. He was interested in politics and served as Allen County Democratic chairman (1934–1936). He was appointed and served as Assistant United States Attorney (1936–1941), as United States Attorney (1941–1946), and as Assistant Attorney-General of the United States (1948–1950), when he resigned and returned to Indiana to campaign for a senatorial nomination that would allow him to challenge Senator Homer Capehart, the then-incumbent from Indiana. Campbell easily won the Democratic nomination and received support from President Truman, but lost the general election in Indiana by some 100,000 votes. He then continued to work in the law firm of Campbell, Livingston, Temple and Dildine, which he had formed in 1944 in Fort Wayne. This firm was dissolved in 1966, and at the time of his death he had a private practice.

Some of the cases supervised by Mr. Campbell were: Axis Sally, treason; Tokyo Rose, treason; Martin James Monti, treason; Herbert John Burgman, treason; J. Parnell Thomas, fraud; twelve Communist party leaders (New York); New York spy grand jury investigation, Hiss-Chambers; Gubitchev and Judith Coplon, espionage.

Alexander M. Campbell and Eleanor E. Church were married on July 5, 1935; they had one son, Thomas Morton, who attended Indiana University at Fort Wayne. Mr. Campbell was a member of the First Christian Church, of which he was an official, and was active in the work of the church in Fort Wayne (Board of Trustees, 1945–55). He was a member of the Indiana University Alumni Association (National President 1939–41); Elks, Moose, Eagles, Kiwanis, and Masonic Organizations; Quest Club, Indiana Saddle Horse Association (President 1957); Shrine (Vice-President International Shrine Horse Patrol); Royal Order of Jesters; and a Director of the Boys' Clubs of America.

Alexander M. Campbell was elected by the State Board of Education on November 12, 1948, as Trustee of Indiana University, succeeding William Kunkel, deceased. Campbell served until 1953. He was a Director of the Indiana University Foundation (1948–53).

Alex bred, raised, trained, and exhibited palomino horses at his ranch in Coesse, Indiana. When Indiana University went to the Rose Bowl in 1968, he and his second wife, Ruby, rode their horses in the Rose Bowl Parade. En route home, they stopped in El Paso, Texas, where Alex had a heart attack and died January 4, 1968, in an El Paso hospital. He was buried at Coesse near his ranch in Whitley County, Indiana.

Donald Carroll Danielson, 1919–
TRUSTEE, 1959–1980
Vice-President of the Board, 1957–1968
President of the Board, 1969–1980

Donald Carroll Danielson, son of Ben Raymond and Freda (Holdhusen) Danielson, was born in Spring Valley, Minnesota, on December 3, 1919. He graduated from Pierre High School in Pierre, South Dakota, and entered Indiana University, where he obtained a B.S. in Education (1942).

He married Patricia Jane Peterson of Indianapolis (B.A. 1945) on April 12, 1947, and they had three daughters: Mary Carroll (Mrs. Michael Hoover Schatzlein, B.S. in Education 1971), Susan Jane (Mrs. Duane Anderson, B.S. in Education 1973) and Amy Elizabeth (Mrs. Ronald Thompson, Jr., B.S. in Business 1980).

Danny, as Mr. Danielson is better known, was an outstanding baseball player at Indiana University and was signed by the Brooklyn Dodgers immediately after his graduation. He played on their Valdosta team in the Florida/Georgia League until he entered the United States Navy V-7 Officers Training Program, graduating as an Ensign from Northwestern University. He served in both the Atlantic and Pacific arenas until 1946, when he was discharged with the rank of Lieutenant, Sr. Grade.

Donald Carroll Danielson

Turning down several offers to return to baseball, Danny opted to return to Indiana University as the Assistant Alumni Secretary in May 1946. In 1948, however, he became the interim coach for the baseball team and also taught a baseball course for physical education majors in the School of Education.

In July 1948 he began a business career as a salesman for New Castle Products, Incorporated, and moved up through the ranks until he was elected President of Modernfold (formerly New Castle Products) in January 1969. In August 1976 Danny changed careers becoming the Senior Vice-President of City Securities Corporation, the oldest and largest investment banking firm in Indiana. He was elected Vice-Chairman of the company in 1981.

During his student days at Indiana University, Danny belonged to the social fraternity Sigma Chi, which he served as President. He was a member of the upper-classmen's honorary, Vice-President of the Sphinx Club, and a member of the Blue Key, a scholastic honorary. He was also the campaign manager of Greek letter organizations for campus elections, a three-year varsity baseball man, and a member of the "I" Men's Association.

Danny's loyalty to Indiana University was not lessened by a summer session of post-graduate work at Purdue.

His social affiliations include the Indiana University Alumni Association (life member), Westwood Country Club, Columbia Club of Indianapolis, Skyline Club of Indianapolis, Downtown Rotary Club of Indianapolis, and Sigma Chi fraternity (life member).

Danny is on the boards of directors of the Indiana/Purdue Foundation; Indiana University Foundation; Indiana Division, Indiana State Chamber of Commerce; Henry County Savings and Loan Association; Indiana Gas Company, Incorporated; City Securities Corporation; Winona Hospital Memorial Foundation; State Republican Citizens Finance Committee; National Fellowship of Christian Athletes; International Institute of Sports; Science and Medicine; American Cancer Society; and Lambda Corporation of Sigma Chi. He is a Republican and an elder in the Presbyterian Church.

Among the honors that have come to Danny are Sagamore of the Wabash, Order of Kentucky Colonels, Confederacy of Indiana Sachews, Zora G. Clevenger Award from the "I" Men's Association (1969), Service Award from Sport Magazine (1970), New Castle Chamber of Commerce "Citizen of the Year" (1972), honorary member of Beta Gamma Sigma, an honor society.

He served on the IU Board of Trustees for twenty-one years (1959–80, and was President of the Board from 1969 to 1980).

Merrill Stamper Davis, 1890–1974
Trustee, 1950–1953; 1959–1962

Merrill Stamper Davis, surgeon of Marion, Grant County, Indiana, was born in Miami, Indiana, March 11, 1890, son of George Washington and Sadie Isabel (Perry) Davis. George Washington Davis graduated from the Eclectic Medical Institute* of Cincinnati in 1890. He began his practice in Miami, but in 1895 he removed to Marion, where Merrill attended grade and high school.

On completing high school Merrill entered Indiana University in the fall of 1908. He had great enthusiasm for atheltics and played varsity football in 1909, 1910, and 1911. Merrill's athletic activity was undertaken against his father's wishes, and, when the older Davis discovered the truth, he withdrew financial support for some of the period his son was in college. Merrill supported himself, in part, by organizing a piano-drum-saxophone group and playing on the Bloomington campus and elsewhere. He was an outstanding saxophone player and teacher. He took part in the organization of the first Indiana State High School Basketball Tournament at Indiana University on March 10, 1911, as a member of the "Booster Club" (a group of students on the IU campus). He was captain of his own basketball team in his senior year (1912).

---

*This school of medicine at a later date became the Eclectic Medical College of Cincinnati. It was founded in 1833, and the last class was graduated in 1929.

Merrill Stamper Davis

In the fall of 1910 Merrill entered the Indiana University School of Medicine. He was graduated on August 30, 1912, with the A.B. degree and on June 21, 1914, with the M.D. degree. On the completion of an internship (1914–1915) at St. Vincent's Hospital, he entered the practice of medicine with his father at Marion.

In April, 1917, he entered the Medical Corps of the United States Army, and in 1918 he was assigned to take a special course in orthopedic surgery at Harvard Medical School. He served as orthopedic surgeon at Fort Sam Houston, Texas, and at Base Hospital 29, Reconstruction Center, Fort Snelling in Minnesota.

In 1919 Merrill returned to practice in Marion, specializing in general and orthopedic surgery. He was a pioneer in the field of industrial surgery and medicine in Indiana.

He was a fellow of the American College of Surgeons and of the International College of Surgeons. Active in local and state medical matters, he had been a trustee of the Marion General Hospital since 1932. He was Past President of the Eleventh Councillor District Medical Society, founder and Past President of the Indiana Bone and Joint Club, Past President of the Grant County Medical Society, orthopedic consultant for the Veterans Administration, surgeon for the New York Central and Nickel Plate Railways, first President of Indiana University School of Medicine Alumni Association, and trustee and Vice-President of the James Whitcomb Riley Memorial Association. He was Secretary of the Surgical Section of the Indiana State Medical Society (1925); orthopedic consultant to the Selective Service System, World War II; Director of Ambulatory Fracture Association (1945–46); and one of the founders and President of Navy League, Marion, Indiana.

In 1913 Merrill married Mary Josephine DeMarcus, of Bloomington, Indiana. They had two sons, Joseph (A.B. 1939, M.D. 1942) and Richard (A.B. 1942, M.D. 1944). Both are graduates of Indiana University and the Indiana University School of Medicine. Joseph served in the Medical Corps of the Navy, and Richard served in the Medical Corps of the Army in World War II. Davis and his two sons organized the Davis Clinic in Marion (1951).

On July 1, 1950, a letter from Governor Schricker announced the election by the State Board of Education of Merrill Stamper Davis as a Trustee of Indiana University to succeed Dr. Dillon Geiger. Dr. Davis was seated on July 21 and served until 1953, when he was replaced by Dr. Dillon Geiger. Dr. Davis was appointed again in 1959 and served until 1962, when he was replaced by Mrs. Harriet Inskeep.

Over the years Davis continued his service to and interest in Indiana University. His interest in music continued throughout his life, and he and Mrs. Davis were staunch supporters of the Music School and The Friends of Music. He received the Distinguished Alumni Award (1963) and the Zora G. Clevenger Award (1969) for contributions to the Indiana University athletics program. When his son, Joseph, also received the Clevenger Award (1980), they became the only father-son combination to have that distinction. He was a life member of the Indiana University Alumni Association and its national President from 1944 to 45. During his tenure a number of constituent alumni societies were originated, and he was a member of the founding committee of the Indiana University School of Medicine Alumni Association. He also belonged to the Varsity Club and the "I" Men's Association. Together with Dr. Cyrus J. Clark (Professor of Medicine), John Van Nuys (Dean of the Medical School), and several other Medical School personnel, Davis orginated the celebration of a Medical School Alumni Day under "the big tent," a tradition that continues in May of each year.

Dr. Davis continued to see patients until five weeks before his death on June 5, 1974, at the University Hospital in Indianapolis. He was buried in Marion, Indiana.

John Ehret Early, 1912–
Trustee, 1965–1971

John Ehret Early, attorney and civic leader, son of John Jubal and Leah Katherine (Robinson) Early, was born in Greenfield, Indiana, on November 6, 1912. He attended public school in Greenfield and then took his A.B. degree in 1934 at DePauw

John Ehret Early

University, following with the LL.B. (J.D.) in 1936 from Indiana University. He was elected President of the Law School Student Body (1935). He has been a practicing attorney in Evansville, Indiana, since 1936, where he had his own firm since 1942 (now Early, Arnold, and Ziemer), having been with Walker and Walker from 1936 to 1942.

John married Ann G. Walker on September 17, 1938, and they had two daughters: Judith Ann (Mrs. Daniel L. Henderson) and Elizabeth Walker (Mrs. Cecil R. Good).

John Early founded and was the first President of the Evansville Legal Aid Society. He holds memberships in Phi Delta Theta, Phi Delta Phi, the Evansville Bar Association (President, 1954), Indiana State Bar Association, American Bar Association, American Judicature Society, Bar Association of the Seventh Federal Circuit, the Elks Lodge, and the Methodist Church. He is a Democrat. John was on the Boards of Directors of the Boehne Hospital (1955–63), Evansville Association for the Blind (1964–68), and Evansville Chamber of Commerce (1967–68). John has twice served as a deputy prosecuting attorney for Vandenburg County and was formerly Chairman of the Young Lawyers section of the Indiana State Bar Association.

Among the honors Early has received was the James Bethel Gresham Freedom Award from the Evansville Bar Association (1964).

Early served on IU's Athletic Committee (1959–62) and was named to the policy committee on the University School (which had a cooperative agreement with Bloomington Metropolitan Schools); he was appointed Trustee of Indiana University and served two consecutive terms, ending in 1971. During his first term as a Trustee, Early served as a member of the Search and Screen Committee for the selection of a new President (1968). During this second term as Trustee, Early made a trip (June 10–July 16, 1969) with Dean Lynne Merritt to visit Indiana University projects in Germany, Afghanistan, Pakistan, Thailand, and Japan under the auspices of MUCIA. He also was a member of the Board of Trustees of the IU Foundation (1967–71).

Jesse Ernest Eschbach II, 1920–
TRUSTEE, 1965–1970

Jesse Ernest Eschbach, attorney and judge, son of Jesse E. and Mary W. (Stout) Eschbach, was born in Warsaw, Indiana, on October 26, 1920. He attended grammar and high schools in Warsaw and entered Indiana University, from which he received his B.S. in 1943. His education was interrupted by service in the Navy (1943 to 1946), in which he held the rank of lieutenant, J.G. Returning to Indiana University, he received the J.D. with distinction in 1949. Jesse married Sara A. Walker on March 15, 1947, and they had two children: Jesse E. III (B.M. with high distinction 1973, M.M. with highest distinction 1975) and Virginia (Mrs. Norman K. Peters, A.B. 1975, M.D. 1980). Mr. Peters also graduated from IU (A.B. 1979).

Immediately upon graduation Jesse joined the firm which became Graham, Rasor, Eschbach, and Harris. He was with this firm until 1960, when he became President of the Endicott Church Furniture Company, where he remained until 1962. Eschbach also served as City Attorney and Deputy Prosecutor of Koseiusko County. In 1962, he became a Judge in the U.S. District Court in northern Indiana and later became Chief Judge of that court (1974).

When Governor Branigan appointed him to the Indiana University Board of Trustees in 1965, Eschbach immediately went on record, following the precedent set by Judge John S. Hastings, as being unwilling to accept the statutory per diem compensation for Trustees. He also served as a member of the Indiana/Purdue Foundation Fort Wayne. During his tenure on the Indiana University Board, he was interested in and tried to help solve some of the student-university problems which emerged during this troubled period. Although he had been appointed to a second term as Trustee in 1968, by February 1970 he found it imperative to resign due to the heavy pressures of his court schedule.

Jesse was a member of the Indiana and American Bar Associations, the American Judicature Society, the Presbyterian Church, the Rotary Club of Warsaw (President in 1955),

Jesse Ernest Eschbach II

Warsaw Chamber of Commerce (President in 1956), and a Trustee of the Donald J. Dalton Foundation, an educational organization (1955-62). For his many civic services he was named Warsaw Man-of-the-Year in 1961 by the *Warsaw Times-Union* and Warsaw Chamber of Commerce.

In November 1981 Judge Eschbach was appointed to the U.S. Court of Appeals for the Seventh Circuit, and his installation took place in Chicago on December 11, 1981.

Paul Lambert Feltus, 1889-1971
Trustee, 1934-47; 1949-57

Paul Lambert Feltus, Monroe County editor, was born in Bloomington, Indiana, December 10, 1889, the son of Henry James and Catherine Ella (Baird) Feltus. The Feltus family was of Scotch-Irish descent. The first generation of the family, one branch of which was related to Alexander Hamilton, settled in New York soon after the establishment of the original colonies. Henry James Feltus I was the first rector of St. Stephen's Episcopal Church in New York City. Paul's father was born in 1845 on Staten Island, New York, and came west shortly before the Civil War to join his father in Cincinnati. He enlisted in the Union Army, later becoming Adjutant of the Thirteenth Indiana Cavalry and serving in many of the major engagements of the war.

After his marriage to Catherine Baird of Terre Haute, Henry J. Feltus came to Bloomington in 1875, where he established the Feltus Printing Company. Here Paul was born, attended the Bloomington schools and, in February 1917, entered Indiana University. His University studies were interrupted by his enlistment in the United States Army in the first World War.

On June 25, 1922, Paul married Lucile Clevenger of Anderson, Indiana (A.B. 1919); they had two daughters: Martha Virginia (Mrs. A. Donald Walstrum, A.B. 1946, MAT 1954) and Paula Lucile (Mrs. Robert A. Hart, B.S. in Education 1956).

Paul had written the scripts for several Hollywood silent films prior to his World War I enlistment. He continued his

Paul Lambert Feltus

writing career along somewhat different lines when he became editor of the *Bloomington Star-Courier* and president of the Feltus Printing Company Inc., (1920). From 1920 to 1965 Paul was editor and publisher of the *Bloomington Star-Courier,* a newspaper recognized many times both nationally and in the state with citations for excellence. In 1965 Paul organized Paul. L. Feltus and Associates, Press Relations-Newspaper Consultants in Bloomington. After the sale of the *Star-Courier,* Feltus became Associate Editor of *The Bloomington Tribune,* a new daily and Sunday newspaper that began publication on September 11, 1966.

From 1921 to 1926 Feltus was a field artillery captain in the Indiana National Guard and was appointed a colonel when he took command of the Fifth Infantry, Indiana State Guard (1941). He later was chosen to be one of the press representatives who witnessed the atomic bomb tests in the Marshall Islands.

Lucile Feltus died March 18, 1934. In November 1943, Mr. Feltus married Thelma Hinkle of Bloomington.

Paul was a member of Sigma Delta Chi, the national journalistic society, and the Sigma Alpha Epsilon social fraternity. He was a life member of the Elks Lodge, a charter member of Burton Woolery Post 18 of the American Legion, a former state secretary of the Kiwanis Club, and a member of both the Reserve Officers' Association and the Wing Club of New York City. He also served as a Director on the Board of the Monroe County State Bank and was President of the Indiana Democratic Editorial Association (1941). He belonged to the Trinity Episcopal Church in Bloomington.

Mr. Feltus served for six years as a member of the Bloomington school board. In 1934 he was elected by the State Board of Education as Trustee of Indiana University to fill an unexpired term. He served four full terms until June 1947. He was appointed again in 1951 and served two more consecutive terms (1951–57). During this period he also was Acting Postmaster of Bloomington (October 1953–April 1955).

Feltus died on February 2, 1971, and is buried in Rose Hill Cemetery.

Robert Edwards Gates

Robert Edwards Gates, 1920–

TRUSTEE, 1969–

Vice-President of the Board, 1975–

Robert Edwards Gates, attorney and civic leader, son of Ralph F. and Helen (Edwards) Gates, was born November 19, 1920, in Columbia City, Indiana. Ralph Gates was Governor of Indiana from 1945 to 1949, after which he returned to the practice of law in his Columbia City firm, joining his son Robert, his brother Benton E., and two cousins. Robert graduated from Columbia City High School and entered Indiana University in 1938, receiving a B.S. (1942) from the School of Business. He was President of his Senior Class. After graduation he spent four years as a Lieutenant in the Navy. Returning from Pacific duty, Robert entered Indiana University's Law School and received his J.D. degree (1949).

On June 9, 1948, he married Harriett Kunkel Brown of Bluffton, Indiana (A.B. in Speech and Hearing 1947), and they had three daughters, all of whom attended Indiana University: Marjorie B. (Mrs. Kenneth Giffin, A.B. in English 1974), Anne E. (Mrs. Kirby Redman, B.S. in Education 1976), and Mary Ellen Gates (who graduated in December 1982 with a degree in Education—teaching Physical Education).

Robert was very active at Indiana University; his many interests are indicated by the variety of organizations to which he belonged: Phi Delta Phi (the legal honorary fraternity); Sigma Alpha Epsilon (social fraternity of which he was President one year); Sphinx Club; Blue Key (recognition society for upperclass males); Skull and Crescent; Union Board. He also served as business manager of the University Theatre, Senior Swimming Manager, and President of the Indiana Memorial Union Board (1941–42). His University ties and interests were continued with a three-year term on the Alumni Council (1956–1959) and the presidency of the Whitley County Varsity Club.

Gates joined the firm of Gates and Gates in June 1949 and has been with it ever since. From 1951 to 1955 he also served as Columbia City Attorney. He is a director of the Farmers

Loan and Trust Company and of the Indiana University/ Purdue University Foundation at Fort Wayne.

Like his father, Robert was active in politics, serving as Whitley County Republican Chairman (1959–1977) and as Fourth District Republican Chairman (1961–1969, 1974–). In addition to his professional memberships in the American, Indiana, and Whitley County (President 1969) Bar Associations, Robert was a member of the Jr. Chamber of Commerce and, later, the Columbia City Chamber of Commerce, the Columbia Club, and the Indiana Society of Chicago. He has held the following offices in the American Legion: Post #98 Commander, Fourth District Commander, State Judge Advocate, State Northern Vice-Commander, State Commander (1957–1958), and National Membership Chairman (1958–1960). He is a member of the IU Foundation Board (1971–) and has served on the Board of Directors of Culver Summer Schools (1972–1975). Gates has twice been awarded The Sagamore of the Wabash (1969 and 1975) and was made a Kentucky Colonel (1969). He is a Presbyterian, belongs to the Masonic Order, including Mizpah Shrine, Rotary (President 1954–1955), Elks, Eagles, Moose, and the VFW Post #2919.

Governor Edgar D. Whitcomb appointed Gates as an Indiana University Trustee in 1969, and he was reappointed for consecutive terms by Governors Bowen and Orr in 1975, 1978, and 1981.

Dillon Donald Geiger, 1907–
Trustee, 1947–1950; 1953–54; 1956–59

Dillon Donald Geiger, Monroe County otolaryngologist, was born September 23, 1907, at Bloomington, Indiana, the son of Walter and Carrie Geiger. He was graduated from the Bloomington High School in June, 1925, and in the fall of that year he entered Indiana University as a premedical student. On the completion of only two years of collegiate work, he was chosen from 458 applicants as a member of the freshman class in the School of Medicine for the year 1927–1928. He was graduated from Indiana University with the degree B.S. in

Dillon Donald Geiger

1929, with the M.D. in 1931, and was elected to membership in Alpha Omega Alpha, the scholastic honor medical society. In June, 1931, he married Louise Mitchum, of Bloomington, 1927 graduate of the School of Music.

After his graduation from the School of Medicine, Dr. Geiger served an internship in the Indianapolis City Hospital (1931-1932). He served as resident in the Indianapolis City Hospital (1932-1933), and did further postgraduate work at the School of Medicine under the late Dr. John F. Barnhill.

In February, 1934, he began the practice of otolaryngology in Bloomington. In 1935 he took a short postgraduate course in otolaryngology in Cook County Hospital, Chicago, and in 1942 another short course at the Presbyterian Hospital Medical Center, Columbia University, New York City. In 1941 Dr. Geiger became a diplomate of the American Board of Otolaryngology and, in the same year, a fellow of the American Academy of Otolaryngology, as well as a member of the Indiana Academy of Otolaryngology. In 1945 he became a fellow of the American College of Surgeons.

In World War II Dr. Geiger attended the Aviation School of Medicine, Randolph Field, Texas. On retiring from service in the Medical Corps of the Army Air Force he held the rank of Major.

Geiger has kept close ties to IU. He has served as President of the Medical Alumni; for several years was a member of the Athletic Committee; he and his wife donated the property for the Musical Arts Center during the 150th Birthday Fund Campaign.

Dr. Geiger is a member of the American, state, and county medical societies; and he served on the IU Hospital staff in Indianapolis, where he lectured on anatomy. He was a member of the Bloomington Hospital staff until his retirement from practice (January 1, 1979), is a past President of the Indiana Medical Association, has served as a consultant to the Monon Railroad, was chairman of the Selective Service Board, and is a Scottish Rite Mason and member of the American Legion.

On June 30, 1947, Dr. Geiger was elected by the State Board of Education as a Trustee of Indiana University, succeeding Paul Feltus, of Bloomington (1947–1950). Dr. Geiger was appointed Trustee again (1953), but served only one year because of his appointment (1954) to the State Toll Road Commission, of which he became Chairman. However, he again served a full term as Trustee from 1956 to 1959.

In 1981 Dr. Geiger received the Distinguished Alumni Service Award.

Harry Lee Gonso, 1948–
Trustee, 1976–

Harry Lee Gonso, lawyer, son of Harry and Amy Helena (Grover) Gonso, was born March 10, 1948, in Findlay, Ohio, where he was graduated from high school in 1966. Harry received a B.S. in Accounting (1970) and a J.D. with honors (1973) from Indiana University. Upon graduation he joined the firm of Bingham, Summers, Welsh, and Spilman in Indianapolis.

At Indiana University Harry was a member of Sigma Alpha Epsilon social fraternity, Indiana University Student Foundation, and Blue Key. He was an All-American in football, having been the quarterback on the Indiana University Rose Bowl team in 1968 while only a sophomore. He was a scholar as well as an athlete, had been on the Dean's List, and was recognized as an Academic All-American with the presentation of the Balfour Award in 1967 and 1968. While in law school he served for two years as Administrative Assistant to Chancellor Herman B Wells and was the first recipient of the "Outstanding Promise" Fellowship.

On September 12, 1970, Harry married Jonni Lauritzen (A.B. 1972, Ph.D. 1977), and they had three children: Christopher Lee (1976), Matthew Henry (1979) and Helen Irene (March 9–April 24, 1982).

Gonso is a member of the Indianapolis, the Indiana, and the American Bar Associations and of the National Association Section of Corporate and Banking Law. He is Secretary of the State Section on Corporate and Banking Law and a Director of the Columbia Club (also its Secretary), and of the Heritage Venture Group, Inc., the Indiana Sports Center, and the

Harry Lee Gonso

Municipal Recreation, Inc. (the entity which manages the Indianapolis Sports Center). He is a past member of the Jaycees and currently belongs to the Indiana University Alumni Association, Varsity Club, "I" Men's Association, Woodstock Club, Penrod Society and the Indianapolis Racquet Club.

He was elected to the Board of Trustees in 1976 and was re-elected for a second term beginning July 1979.

Carl M. Gray, 1895–
TRUSTEE, 1967—1975

Carl M. Gray, lawyer, philanthropist, and civic leader, son of John D. and Emma Louise (Rudolph) Gray, was born September 3, 1895, in Portersville, Indiana, the birthplace of his parents. He attended school in Petersburg and entered Indiana University in September, 1915. With the advent of World War I, he left for the Army, working his way through the ranks to become a First Lieutenant in the Adjutant General's office by the time he left the service. He returned to law school in February 1919 and completed courses in fifteen resident months. Unable to reconcile a difference of opinion with the Dean of the Law School as to whether Carl needed eight or twelve hours more work, he left Indiana University and went into law practice. When he was home on furlough from the U.S. Army (November 19, 1917) he was admitted to the Bar and has practiced law in Petersburg since November 1, 1920. However, in 1961, after forty years of practice, Gray re-enrolled in the Law School and passed the examinations to earn the LL.B. Degree.

On February 26, 1927, Carl married Eulala Myers of Monroe City, Indiana. They had one son who died in infancy.

Gray was Prosecuting Attorney for Pike and Dubois counties (1923–1925) and a Senator in the Indiana General Assembly (1927 and 1929). While in the Senate, he assisted in writing the law establishing a statewide property tax levy and a bonding authority for construction of academic facilities at state universities. He has assisted in writing other legislation both at home and in England, including rules and regulations on

Carl M. Gray

stripmining in Wales and a new judicial article for the Indiana Constitution (ratified 1970).

Although he was President (1957-1974) and Chairman of the Board (1951-1957) of the First National Bank of Petersburg (he became a Director in 1947 and held that position until he gave up the Presidency in 1974), his primary interest was the law and its associated organizations. He was the organizer and first Chairman of the Trial Lawyers Section (1957-1959) of the Indiana State Bar Association. Within the latter organization he held membership on innumerable committees and commissions, served as its President (1944-1945) and Chairman of the House of Delegates (1963-1966), and in October, 1966, was given their Distinguished Service Award. Gray is a Fellow in the American College of Trial Lawyers, the American College of Probate Counsel, and the Indiana Bar Foundation. He also is a member of the Pike County Bar Association, Indiana State Bar Association, American Bar Association, Seventh Circuit Court of Appeals Bar Association, Indiana Judicial Council (1976-), American Judicature Society, Federation of Insurance Counsel, National Association of Railroad Trial Counsel, and the Academy of Law and Science.

In January, 1967, Gray was appointed to the Indiana University Board of Trustees to fill the remaining term of Judge Donald A. Rogers (who resigned to avoid possible conflict of interest after he became a judge) and then was reappointed to full terms in 1969 and 1972.

Gray is a Mason, an elder and Trustee of the Main Street Presbyterian Church in Petersburg, a past President and former member of the Board of Trustees of the Westminister Foundation at Indiana University (1954-1960), a member of the Board of Trustees of Vincennes University Foundation (1961-), Director of Oakland City College Foundation (1975, and Emeritus Chairman of its Board), a member of the Indiana University Foundation Board of Directors (1970-). He is also Lt. Governor of the Kiwanis Club (1932), past Commander of Conrad Post #179 of the American Legion (1923, 1938, 1939), and a member of Sigma Alpha Epsilon social fraternity. He has been active in the Boy Scouts (for which he built the Worship

Center near Camp Arthur), was an honorary member of Buffalo Trace Boy Scouts Council, and has sponsored a Little League team every year since the program was organized in 1958. In 1958, with Mrs. Gray, he established the yearly Gray Citizenship Award for 4-H Club boys and girls.

In February 1978, Gray became the first county-seat lawyer ever to receive the distinguished fifty-year award of the Fellows of the American Bar Foundation. Other honors that have come to Carl include the Sagamore of the Wabash Award from the Indiana governor (1966, 1975); Indiana University Distinguished Alumni Award (1976); William Henry Harrison Award from Vincennes University; Distinguished Service Award and Outstanding Service Award (1968) from the IU Foundation; honorary membership in Knox County Bar Association, IU Law School, Indianapolis, Distinguished Practitioner-in-Residence (1973); and an honorary LL.D. from Indiana University (1981).

The Carl M. and Eulala M. Gray Trial Advocacy Endowment Fund was created by Carl Gray in September 1978 after the death of Mrs. Gray on March 12, 1978. Income for this fund goes to further the education of law students in the area of trial advocacy at both the Bloomington and Indianapolis Law Schools of Indiana University. At the IU Law Schools, the Carl M. Gray Chair in Advocacy (Indianapolis) and the Carl M. Gray Advocacy Program (Bloomington) were established in his honor.

Even with all of the foregoing involvements, Carl has found time to breed fine bird dogs and has been an avid hunter of quail, pheasant, duck and goose, all of which he can prepare in a proper Southern Indiana manner. He also finds time to attend most of the IU football and basketball games at Bloomington.

James Walter Gray, 1960–
STUDENT TRUSTEE, 1981–1983

James Walter Gray, son of Ennis (of New York City) and Kathleen (Clune) Gray (of Long Island, NY) was born in Arlington, Virginia, on June 3, 1960. He attended local schools and then

James Walter Gray

spent two years at Wilton High School in Wilton, Connecticut, until his family moved to Carmel, Indiana, where he completed his high school studies (1978). He played basketball and baseball at Wilton High School and worked in the Pro Shop of Woodland Country Club.

He matriculated at Indiana University in 1978 where he joined Phi Kappa Psi social fraternity and was elected to Blue Key and the Alpha Lambda Delta and Phi Eta Sigma (freshman scholarship organizations). He majored in Law and Public Policy in the School of Public and Environmental Affairs (B.S. in Public Affairs, August 1982).

Gray has been active in the IU Student Association since 1978 (Senator 1979–1980, Vice-President 1980–81), was a member of the Board of Aeons, and has served as the student *ex-officio* member of the Bloomington and University Faculty Councils.

His political leanings are toward the Democratic Party.

Carolyn Prickett Gutman, 1932–
Trustee, 1974–

Carolyn Prickett Gutman, civic leader and educator, daughter of Ward Delwin and Margaret Marie (Harris) Prickett was born June 22, 1932, in Mishawaka, Indiana, where her mother served as mayor (1963–79). Carolyn attended grammar and high schools in Mishawaka and then entered Indiana University, obtaining a B.A. (1954) and later an M.S. in Education (1962).

On September 3, 1955, Carolyn married Phillip Edward Gutman (B.S. 1952, J.D. 1957) and they had three children: Phillip Edward, Jr. (B.S. Business 1980), Gretchen Kay (currently, 1982, a student at IU), and Kurt Alan Gutman.

While an undergraduate, Carolyn was a member of the IU Student Foundation, was one of six women chosen by the Association of Women Students to serve on the first all-student Union Board (1953–1954), and was President of Alpha Phi sorority (1953–1954). She was a Residence Hall Counselor (1954–1955) and the Activities Advisor in the Dean of Students' Office (1955–1957).

Carolyn Prickett Gutman

Active in both civic and educational endeavors, Carolyn has been on the Board of Directors of the YWCA, Associated Churches of Fort Wayne, Pre-School Center for Hearing Handicapped (1969–), and Big Brothers-Big Sisters of Fort Wayne (1976–); on the Advisory Boards of Foster Grandparents (1972–75), IU-PU at Fort Wayne (1973–) and Fort Wayne Community Schools (1976–78); on the Board of Trustees of Parkview Memorial Hospital (1982–85), and Aldergate United Methodist Church (1973–75, Administrative Board 1980–84, Vice-President 1982, Pastor/Parish Relations Committee 1981–83); President of the Fort Wayne Panhellenic Council (1959–60); member of the Junior League of Fort Wayne (1962–   , President 1971–72); member of the Fort Wayne Bicentennial Committee (chairman of Volunteers, 1974–76). She has also been Vice-President or President in alternating years since 1974 of the IU-PU Foundation (currently President, 1982–83) and founder and President (1975–81) of the Friends of Indiana-Purdue at Fort Wayne.

In 1978 she was given the Ursa Major Award from Alpha Phi sorority, a national recognition for service and achievement in the community. She received the Ralph E. Broyles Medal from the IU Alumni Association for unique and significant contributions to Indiana University in Fort Wayne (1979).

Carolyn holds memberships in the Fort Wayne Museum of Art, Friends of Music, Hoosier Salon Patrons Association, Indianapolis Museum of Art, State Assembly Women's Club, Fort Wayne Zoological Society, Indianapolis Children's Museum, IU Alumni Association (life membership), IU Alumni Club of Fort Wayne, Well House Society, Woodburn Guild, James Whitcomb Riley Hospital Association, and Fox Island Alliance.

She is a Republican and her husband Phillip, a state senator (1968–76), was President *pro tempore* of the Indiana Senate (1971–76).

Carolyn was appointed by the Governor to serve on the IU Board of Trustees (1974) and has twice been reappointed to consecutive terms (1977 and 1980).

John Simpson Hastings, 1898-1977
TRUSTEE, 1936-1959
President of the Board, 1951-1959

John Simpson Hastings, lawyer of Daviess County, was born in Washington, Indiana, June 30, 1898, the son of Elmer Ellsworth and Bertha Jane (Garten) Hastings. The family is of English descent, and the original settlement was made at Philadelphia in the early eighteenth century by John Hastings, a member of William Penn's Society of Friends. At Philadelphia on May 13, 1735, Joshua Hastings was born, the first of John's American-born ancestors. His son, Joshua, Jr., was born July 31, 1769. He moved to North Carolina, and to him was born Howell Hastings, on May 2, 1805, John's great-grandfather, who moved to Daviess County, Indiana, where the family continues to reside. John was of the seventh generation of his family in America.

John Hastings attended the grade and high schools of Washington, Indiana. He was graduated in 1916, and in the fall of that year entered Indiana University. He completed two full years of collegiate work in June, 1918, at which time he entered the United States Military Academy at West Point as a cadet, on appointment of Congressman Oscar Bland. The class was graduated in June, 1920.

John received the B.S. degree from the Military Academy and a commission as a Second Lieutenant of field artillery in the Regular Army. He served fifteen months at Fort Knox, Kentucky, where he became a First Lieutenant. He graduated from the basic fire arms school at Fort Knox in August, 1921, and resigned to complete his interrupted university course.

Returning to Indiana University, he entered the School of Law and was in uninterrupted residence for twenty-seven months, completing the work for the LL.B. degree, December, 1923, although he was not graduated until June 1924. In January, 1924, he began the practice of law in Washington, Indiana, in the firm Allen, Hastings, and Allen. On June 2, 1925, he married Mary Esther Smiley, (A.B., Northwestern

John Simpson Hastings

University, 1924), and they had twin sons, William Elmer and James Roland, born March 12, 1937. Both sons attended Indiana University, and James received an A.B. (1960).

Mr. Hastings was the winner of the Bryan prize in 1918, was a member of the Order of Coif (national law honor society), and was the recipient of the Gamma Eta Gamma 1924 award for the highest scholastic average of the senior law class. He was President of Aeons, a member of the Union Board, and took an effective part in the Memorial Campaign. He served for two years as President of the Alumni Council and had also served as President of the Alumni Association.

In 1936 he was elected by the alumni as a Trustee of Indiana University, to fill the term of Mr. Fesler, which expired July 1, 1938. He served consecutive terms for a total of twenty-three years (President, 1950–59).

Hastings also was a director of the Indiana University Foundation and served as the Foundation's Vice-President (1951). He was an honorary member of the Board from 1969 until his death. He also was an honorary life member of the Riley Hospital Board of Governors since 1969. He presided over the State Board of Law Examiners (1951) of which he was a member for five years. He was appointed a Judge of the United States Court of Appeals in Chicago (1957) by President Dwight D. Eisenhower and served as Chief Judge of the Seventh Circuit (1959–68). He retired to Senior Judge status in 1969.

In 1948 the Law Club, which comprised the entire student body of the Law School, established a new award, the Indiana University School of Law Gavel Award, which was to be presented annually to the individual who had contributed the most to the Law School and its student enrollment, and was to be determined by the senior class each year. The first recipient of this award was Hastings.

Other honors acquired by John were an honorary LL.D. from Indiana University (1959) and another from Northwestern University (1961), and the Lincoln Academy of Illinois law award (1967).

Hastings was a member of the American Law Institute; the Daviess County, Illinois, Indiana, Seventh Circuit, and

Chicago Bar Associations; American Judicature Society; American Colleges of Trial Lawyers (Fellow); American Bar Foundation; Chicago West Point Society; Phi Delta Phi law fraternity; Order of the Coif; and Phi Beta Kappa. He also was a member of the American Legion, Masons, Rotary, Union League Club, and Standard Club, and was a Republican. He was active in the Methodist Church while in Washington, Indiana, and served on the Board of Sessions of the Presbyterian Church in Chicago.

Hastings died February 9, 1977, in a Chicago Hospital and was interred in Washington, Indiana. An endowed professorship was established in his name in 1977.

Walter Edward Helmke, 1901–1976
Trustee, 1954–1956

Walter Edward Helmke, lawyer, politician and civic leader, the son of Herman and Mary (Engel) Helmke, was born on December 17, 1901, in Fort Wayne, Indiana. He married Wilma L. Wehrenberg of Fort Wayne on June 3, 1926. They had three children: Walter P., Mary Ann (Mrs. Charles Scheele of Fort Wayne), and Carolyn Louise (Mrs. Charles Stoltz of Las Vegas, Nevada). Walter's son, Walter P. Helmke (A.B. 1950, J.D. Valparaiso 1952), a Fort Wayne attorney and former State Senator, and one grandson, W. Paul Helmke (A.B. 1970 and President of the Indiana University Student Body in 1969–1970; J.D. Yale 1973), became partners in the law firm of Helmke, Philips, and Beams in Fort Wayne. Both daughters attended Indiana University but neither graduated as they left school to marry before they finished their degree work.

Walter attended St. Paul's Lutheran School and was graduated in 1920 from Central High School, where he had been on the debating team. He then attended Indiana University, studying literature and law, and received an LL.B. degree in 1925. At Indiana University he was President of the Phi Kappa Psi social fraternity, a member of the debating team (1922–1923), and Instructor of Public Speaking and Debating (1923–1924) and the winner of the Niezer Medal in

Walter Edward Helmke

Speech. He also held membership in Phi Delta Phi (honorary legal fraternity) and Tau Kappa Alpha (honorary debating fraternity).

Following graduation in 1925, he was admitted to the Indiana Bar and to practice in the Indiana Supreme and Appellate Courts as well as in the United States District Court for Indiana. He was a member and later president of the Allen County Bar Association. His foray into politics led him to win the office of Prosecuting Attorney (1930–1931) and of City Attorney of Fort Wayne (1934–1937). In the 1934 primary he was a candidate for Congress but was defeated, as he was in 1948 when he was a candidate for Governor at the Republican State Convention. He served as a Republican delegate to that convention as well as to the Republican National Conventions in 1948 and 1952. Walter continued to serve as a Republican delegate to the State Convention for twenty years. He was an authority on city government and had served as President of the National Institute of Municipal Law Officers. He also was the Honorary Consul for the Dominican Republic (1956–76).

Active in civic affairs, he served as Director of the Chamber of Commerce (1967–1969) and was a founder and first President of the Fort Wayne Civic Symphony. He held memberships in the Indianapolis Columbia Club, the Fort Wayne Country, Quest and Summit Clubs. Walter was appointed an Indiana University Trustee for the 1954–1956 term. He was one of those instrumental in establishing the Indiana University/Purdue University Campus at Fort Wayne in 1961, and he later (1962–1976) served on the Board of Directors of the Indiana/Purdue Foundation at Fort Wayne. In 1973 Walter was awarded the honorary LL.D. by Indiana University at the Fort Wayne commencement. He was on the Board of Governors (1970–1976) of the James Whitcomb Riley Hospital Association.

Walter Helmke was active in St. Paul's Lutheran Church, having been Chairman of his congregation and President of the International Walther League (1933–1934), a Lutheran youth organization.

Among the Boards of Directors on which Helmke sat were: Jefferson National Life Insurance Company; Jefferson Corporation; American Precast Concrete, Incorporated (Indianapolis); Burnside, Incorporated (Columbus, Indiana); Driftwood Gravel, Incorporated (Edinburgh, Indiana); Kokomo Ready-Mix Concrete; Indiana Ready Mixed Concrete, Incorporated (Fort Wayne, Indiana); and the Foellinger Foundation, Incorporated, (Fort Wayne, Indiana). In 1975, at Founders Day observances in Fort Wayne, he was awarded the Ralph E. Broyles Medal, given annually by the Allen County Indiana University Alumni Club in memory of the late Chancellor for unique and significant contributions to Indiana University at Fort Wayne. In September 1977 the new library on the IU/PU campus in Fort Wayne was dedicated and named the Walter E. Helmke Library in honor of his contributions to the Fort Wayne Campus.

Walter Helmke died of a heart attack in the Parkview Hospital on February 4, 1976 and was buried in Lindenwood Cemetery in Fort Wayne.

George Washington Henley, 1890-1965
Trustee, 1945-1951

George Washington Henley, lawyer and legislator of Monroe County, was born in Washington, D.C., May 13, 1890, the son of George Washington and Flora (Abell) Henley, both of English descent. The Henley ancestor in America, Patrick Henley, came from Henley-on-Thames, England, and settled in Albemarle County, North Carolina, in early colonial days.

The great-grandson of Patrick was Henry Henley, who married Martha Saunders, February 2, 1794. The Henley family had become Quakers. The youngest son of Henry and Martha was Joseph, the great-grandfather of George Henley, trustee of Indiana University. Henry Henley died, and his widow, Martha, moved to Paoli, a strong Quaker settlement, where she became the second wife of Jonathan Lindley. Joseph Henley married Mary Ann Lindley, one of the descendants of Thomas Lindley, brother of Jonathan. So we find George Henley, related by marriage and blood to

George Washington Henley

Jonathan Lindley, one of the first appointees to the Board of Trustees of Indiana University.

Henry Henley, the second son of Joseph and Mary Ann, grew up in the Quaker community at Paoli, attended the local schools, and later attended Earlham College. During the Civil War Henry enlisted and was made captain of a company of Indiana Volunteer Infantry, a company of the Wilder Brigade. He is credited with the detection and arrest of the leaders of the Knights of the Golden Circle.

Shortly after the close of the war, Henry moved with his family to Bloomington, where he became one of the pioneer stone men of Indiana. Here his son, George W., began and completed his schooling and later entered Indiana University, where he was graduated in 1880. Soon after his graduation, this George W. Henley (father of George, the trustee) was appointed to a position in the War Department in Washington, D.C. He was later transferred to the Office of the Surgeon General. In 1884 he married Flora Abell, of Maryland.

In 1895 George W. Henley brought his family back to Bloomington where George, Jr.'s education was begun and where he had some of the same teachers who had instructed his father. George entered Indiana University on June 24, 1909, a few weeks after being graduated from the Bloomington High School. In the University he was interested in various student activities. He was a director of the Indiana Union in the second year of the existence of that organization. During the years 1911, 1912, and 1913 he was a director of the *Indiana Revue*. He was also a member of the Sphinx Club; a member of the Phi Delta Phi, honorary legal fraternity; a member of the Phi Kappa Psi, social fraternity; and a life member of the Indiana Union.

George was graduated with the A.B. degree (1913) and the LL.B. degree (1914). On graduation he began to practice law in the office of his uncle, Joseph Henley. After the death of his uncle in 1924, he was alone in his practice (except for nine years, 1926 to 1935) until 1949 when he became the senior member of Henley and Bunger.

In 1937 he became a member of the lower house of the Indiana legislature and served in every subsequent session through 1947. In 1943 he was majority leader of the House and served again in that capacity in 1945 and 1947. He was a member of the Indiana Commission on Interstate Cooperation; of the Indiana Legislative Advisory Commission; of the national bill-drafting committee, Council of State Governments; and of the American, Indiana, and local bar associations.

In 1917 George married Elba Fickel (A.B. 1913). They had two daughters: Natalie (Mrs. Gordon W. Hamilton; A.B. 1946, A.M. 1950) and Georgabell (Mrs. Douglas Moffat; A.B. 1950, A.M. 1953).

On July 1, 1940, he was appointed attorney to the Board of Trustees. On June 27, 1945, the State Board of Education elected him as Trustee of Indiana University for a term of three years, beginning July 1, 1945, and re-elected him in 1948, for a term ending in 1951.

In 1956, when the Henleys made an extensive trip to England, George had a chance to attend a session of the House of Commons, and both he and his wife were entertained by Prime Minister Macmillan at No. 10 Downing Street.

Governor George Craig appointed Henley to fill an unexpired term on the Indiana Supreme Court (1955). For many years he served as general counsel for Indiana University, Bloomington Consolidated Schools, Showers Brothers Company, Fagan Stone Company, Graham Motor Sales Company, RCA., Pennsylvania Railroad, Outdoor Advertising Association of Indiana, and many others.

George was director of the Monon Railroad, Indiana Bell Telephone Company, Public Service Company, Showers Brothers, and Fagan Brothers Stone Company. He maintained an active interest in many local organizations such as the Kiwanis Club (past President), Elks Lodge (past Exalted Ruler), Masonic Lodge, Scottish Rite, Indianapolis Press Club, Indiana Society of Chicago, James Whitcomb Riley Association, and the First Methodist Church.

His primary hobbies were stamp collecting and railroads, although he also was an ardent drama and music fan as well. The stamp collection which he started as a youth became one of the most important specialized collections of United States stamps in Indiana.

Henley died in Bloomington on February 19, 1965.

Willis Hickam, 1894–1978
TRUSTEE, 1953–1965
President of the Board, 1959–1965

Willis Hickam, lawyer, was one of three sons born to Willis and Sally (Meek) Hickam in Spencer, Indiana. Willis Sr. was a lawyer in Spencer when his son was born on May 3, 1894. The latter married Ruth Elliott on February 4, 1919, and they had two children: a son Elliott and a daughter, Jane G. (Mrs. Joel Grizzell).

Willis attended Spencer High School and obtained his LL.B. at Indiana University (1918). He then served in the United States Army during World War I and later became active in the American Legion. Leaving the army, Willis established his law practice in Spencer and in 1952 became a Director and Vice-President of the Owen County State Bank. He also was a Director of the Owen County Savings and Loan Association. From 1953–1957 he served as a member of the Indiana Commission on State Tax and Financing Policy. He was a member of the American, Indiana State, and Owen County Bar Associations, a Fellow of the American College of Trial Lawyers since 1954, a Fellow of the American Bar Foundation since 1963, a member of the Board of Managers of the Indiana State Bar Association (1938–1940), and a member of the Bar Association of the Seventh Federal Circuit.

Hickam was a Presbyterian, a Democrat, and held membership in the Masons, Elks, Phi Kappa Psi social fraternity, Phi Delta Phi law fraternity, and the Cataract Yacht Club.

Before becoming an Indiana University Trustee, Willis had served as a part-time Law School instructor, teaching Dean Gavit's "Procedure" course during the second semester of 1948–1949, while Dean Gavit was on sabbatical leave. In 1953, Willis was appointed a Trustee and then reappointed each three years until his final appointment culminated in 1965. He was elected President of the Board in 1959 and served in that office until 1965. He also served as a Director of the Indiana University/Purdue Foundation at Fort Wayne and was a member of the Board of Governors of the James Whitcomb Riley Memorial Association (1971–1978). After retiring from

Willis Hickam

the Indiana University Board of Trustees in November 1965, Willis, who had been serving as one of the three Trustee representatives to the Indiana University Foundation Board, was elected to that Board to fill a vacancy.

Following in the footsteps of another distinguished Hoosier relative, his brother Lt. Colonel Horace M. Hickam (for whom Hickam Field, Hawaii was named), Willis received several prestigious awards both from his alma mater and his law associations. In May 1966 the Sigma Delta Chi presented him with the Big Wheel Award and, in 1967, Indiana University awarded him the honorary LL.D. In 1971 he was the recipient of the "Presidential Citation" from the Indiana State Bar Association.

Although Willis lived most of his life in Spencer, he had moved to Bloomington when he became ill, shortly before he died on February 21, 1978. He was survived by his wife, son Elliott, daughter Jane G. Grizzell, his brother Hubert (a nationally known trial lawyer in Indianapolis who died a few months later on May 30, 1978), and his sister Morna (Hickam) Knipe. He was buried at Riverside Cemetery in Spencer.

Glen Raymond Hillis, 1891–1965

TRUSTEE, 1953–1954

Glen Raymond Hillis, a Kokomo lawyer, farmer, school teacher, and businessman, was born December 9, 1891, in Howard County, Indiana, the son of Harrison N. and Sarah (Stevenson) Hillis. The family can truly be called "Hoosier" since Glen's thrice-great-grandfather came down the Ohio River and settled in an area on its north bank (in what is now known as Jefferson County) before Indiana was a state. He cleared a tract of land on which he lived until 1818. All of the male descendents of this Hillis pioneer farmer continued to be farmers, including Glen, who owned and operated a 160-acre farm in Howard County and maintained his home on an adjacent tract of land until he moved to Kokomo. He also operated his wife's 90-acre farm and a 66-acre farm left by his

Glen Raymond Hillis

mother. Glen had one sister and was the youngest of four brothers.

Hillis worked his way through Kokomo High School by carrying a milk route and working on his father's farm and at odd jobs around Kokomo. After graduating from high school, he taught in the county schools of Howard County, being appointed principal of the West Middleton High School where he also coached the basketball team. By working all winter and attending Indiana University in the spring and summer terms, Glen earned entry into Indiana University's Law School. His schooling was interrupted for two years by World War I, when he enlisted in the Army and became a member of the famous Rainbow Division, serving in many combat engagements in France. He attained the rank of Sergeant by the time he was discharged. His army experience carried him into American Legion affairs, and he later became a member of the Legion's Executive Committee. By combining work with study following his Army stint, Glen finally won his law degree from Indiana University in 1925 and was a practicing lawyer in Howard County until he retired. He was a member of both the Indiana and American Bar Associations.

At Indiana University he was active in discussion groups (debating), as they were then called, and the 1919 *Daily Student* records his participation in a number of such debates during his sophomore year. He also was a member of Phi Delta Phi and Lambda Chi Alpha fraternities.

On November 11, 1920, Glen married his high-school sweetheart Bernice Haynes, whose father, Elwood Haynes, was the inventor of an automobile. They had a daughter, Margaret Hillis, and three sons, Elwood, Robert, and Joseph. Elwood the eldest, is now (1982) a member of the House of Representatives from Indiana. Margaret received her bachelor's degree from Indiana University in 1947, and in 1972 was awarded an honorary doctorate for her work in choral conducting. Glen also was interested in choral work and was President of the American Concert Choir and of Choral Foundation, Incorporated.

Hillis was prominent in Republican affairs for many years. Although not a "professional politician," he was twice elected

Howard County Prosecutor and was the unsuccessful Republican candidate for Governor in 1940.

He was active in community welfare work and for years served as the Chairman of the American Legion National Child Welfare Division. His interest extended to students at all levels; the Hayworth High School was built on the land he donated, a tract adjoining his boyhood home. He served for twenty-five years as Trustee of Butler University, which awarded him an honorary doctor of laws in 1941; his brief tenure as a Trustee for Indiana University was an active one; and his departure because of poor health was a great loss to the University. His community activities also included work with the Red Cross, YMCA, and the Community Chest. The family was Presbyterian and regularly attended the Kokomo Presbyterian Church. Glen's fraternal affiliations included the Masonic Lodge and the Elks.

Indicative of his wide interests and great energy is the list of positions he had to resign, in addition to that of Indiana University Trustee, when his health deteriorated: To the activities of his own law firm, Marshall, Hillis and Hillis, must be added the chairmanship of the Boards of the Union Bank and Trust Company, the First Federal Savings and Loan Association of Kokomo, and the Dirilyte Company of America. He also was President and Director of Mason Motors, Incorporated, and the attorney for the city schools of Kokomo.

Glen Hillis died October 19, 1965, and was buried in Memorial Park Cemetery in Kokomo.

Harriett Simmons Inskeep, 1926–

Trustee, 1962–1971

Harriett (Simmons) Inskeep, civic leader, daughter of Joseph Levi and Mary (Markley) Simmons, was born in Bluffton, Indiana, on August 11, 1926. Harriett graduated from high school in Bluffton and then attended Christian College in Columbia, Missouri, obtaining an Associate of Arts degree in 1946. She then entered Indiana University and obtained an A.B. (1948) and an M.A. in Government (1955), having served

Harriett Simmons Inskeep

as a Graduate Research Assistant in the Bureau of Government Research at Indiana University (1948-1949). A member of Kappa Alpha Theta (social sorority) she later became a member of Tri Kappa (a philanthropic sorority).

On September 3, 1949, she married Richard Glenn Inskeep (B.S. 1950), now (1982) President and Publisher of the *Fort Wayne Journal-Gazette* and Chairman of the Board of Fort Wayne Newspapers, Inc. They have four children: Julia Ann (Mrs. John D. Walda, A.B. 1972, M.S.W. 1974; Mr. Walda, A.B. 1971, J.D. 1975), Joseph Glenn, Thomas Richard, and Stephen Simmons. All three boys are working on degrees at Indiana University.

Mrs. Inskeep was the first appointed woman Trustee. In July 1962, Governor Matthew E. Welsh recommended her appointment, and she was reappointed for two more consecutive terms by Governor Roger Branigan. Her interest in education has been long standing. Before her appointment as a Trustee of Indiana University, she served as chairman of the Fort Wayne Advisory Committee on School Reorganization, and as a charter member of the Committee of Twenty-Four (chairman 1973-82) in Fort Wayne (a bi-racial study group). She also has served as a member of: the American Council of Education's Special Committee to study campus tensions, the National Commission on Accrediting's Advisory Committee on Teacher Education, the National Association of Governing Boards (1963-71), the Indiana Advisory Commission on Academic Facilities (1962-71), the Liaison Committee on Medical Education (1972-78, the national accrediting body for medical schools in the U.S. and Canada), and the National Educational Commission for Foreign Medical Graduates (1976-80).

She continues her interest in education and currently (1982) is serving on the Board of Visitors for the School of Public and Environmental Affairs at Indiana University. In alternating years she has been Vice-President and President of the Indiana University/Purdue Foundation in Fort Wayne since 1968.

Harriett is a Democrat, a member of the Junior League of Fort Wayne and of the First Presbyterian Church. She also served as Charter Director and Secretary of the Indiana

Forum, as Metropolitan chairman of the United Way in Fort Wayne, as a member of the Indiana Public Television Review Committee, as State co-chair of ERA Indiana, and as director of a number of civic agencies.

In 1969 Harriett was selected for honorary membership in Indiana University's Mortar Board (a senior women's honorary) and for membership in Delta Kappa Gamma (a women's educational honorary) in 1972. In April 1978 she was presented with the Broyles Medal for outstanding service to Indiana University at Fort Wayne's Founders Day ceremonies.

Donald Ray Lash, 1912–
Trustee, 1970–1972

Donald Ray Lash, former FBI Special Agent and civic leader, son of Brandon and Pearl (Landis) Lash, was born August 15, 1912, in Bluffton, Indiana. The family moved to Auburn, Indiana, and Donald was graduated from Auburn High School in 1933. He entered Indiana University where he obtained a B.S. (1938) and an M.S. (1940).

Donald married Margaret Mendenhall (a former Indiana University student) on June 18, 1938, and they had three children: Russell Earl (B.S. 1962, Business), David Ray (B.M.E. 1964, Ed.D. in Higher Education 1975), and Marguerite Sue (B.S. 1972 in Radio and TV at Purdue University). Both of the boys followed their father by joining the FBI.

At Indiana, Lash was a member of the 1936 Olympic team that went to Berlin. He had won the NCAA 500-meter race that same year. He was the first American to run two miles in under nine minutes, and was an All-American in track and a national AAU champion in cross-country (1934, 35, and 36). He won the 5000 meter (1938) and received the James E. Sullivan Award (1938). Later he was elected to the Helms All-Time Hall of Fame for track and to the U.S. Track and Field Hall of Fame (1974).

After twenty-one years of service with the FBI, Don retired in 1963 to become the Director of the Resource and Training Center of the Fellowship of Christian Athletes in Marshall,

Donald Ray Lash

Indiana. He was well known throughout the world for his interest and work with youth. He is a member of Delta Chi social fraternity, "I"-Men's Association, the Association of Former FBI Agents, and the Methodist Church. His civic activities have included the Chairmanships of the Marion County Heart Fund and of the Indiana Mental Health Association. He was given the Sagamore of the Wabash (1979) by Governor Bowen.

He was elected to serve as a Trustee in 1970 but regretfully resigned in December 1972 upon his election to the Indiana General Assembly. He served in the House of Representatives for ten consecutive years.

Clarence William Long, 1917–
Trustee, 1975–

Clarence William Long, accountant and civic leader, son of Adam and Alice A. (Weschke) Long, was born in Hartford City, Indiana, on April 17, 1917. He attended local schools through high school and entered Indiana University's Business School from which he obtained a B.S. in 1939.

On August 8, 1940, he married Mildred L. Bernhardt of Evansville, Indiana (Indiana University, B.S. 1939), and they had three children: William Randall (D.D.S. 1969), David John (Georgetown University, J.D. 1974) and Bruce Allen (DePauw, A.B. 1975; University of Chicago, MBA 1977).

Although Long did not get his CPA until 1940, he was employed by Ernst and Ernst in 1939 when he graduated. In 1953 he became a partner in charge of the Indianapolis office.

Clarence was a Junior Achiever and served as President of the local chapter (1957–1959), Chairman of the Midwest Region (1960), and member of the National Executive Board and the Board of Directors (1960–1965). He has continued to be interested in civic affairs and has served as a Director of the Indiana Chamber of Commerce Board of Directors (1974–1979) and of the United Way of Greater Indianapolis Board of Directors (1957–1978).

An art collector, he also has been a Trustee of the In-

Clarence William Long

dianapolis Art Association (1967–) and President of the Indianapolis Museum of Art (1977–1982). Long also holds membership in the Indiana University Academy of Alumni Fellows, Indiana and National Association of CPA's, American Institute of CPA's, Beta Alpha Psi honorary fraternity, Alpha Kappa Psi professional business fraternity, the Masonic order, Indiana Society of Chicago, Delta Chi social fraternity, and the Columbia Club, where he has been on the Board of Directors (1971–1973, 1975–1977; Vice-President of the Board 1972–1973; and President 1976). He attends the Lutheran Church and is a Republican.

Long was appointed Trustee in 1975 and was reappointed for consecutive terms in 1978 and 1981.

Robert Anthony Lucas, 1922–
Trustee, 1967–1970

Robert Anthony Lucas, lawyer, son of Blaz Andrew and Florence (Wilson) Lucas, was born in Gary, Indiana, on February 7, 1922. On his mother's side he is a fifth generation Indianan, his great, great grandmother, Rachel Michael, having been born in Carroll County in 1820. Robert's father, Blaz, was born in Croatia and came with his mother to the United States when he was six-months old to join his father in Calumet, Michigan. Robert's father obtained a law degree from Valparaiso University in 1911 and set up his law practice in Gary. Robert graduated with honors from Horace Mann High School in Gary (1939) and then entered Indiana University, where he obtained his B.S. with honors in the Business School. He was President of the 1943 graduating class.

After graduation, Robert entered the United States Army and served in the Transportation Corporation, spending two years in Europe and reaching the rank of Captain by the time he was discharged in 1946. He then returned to Indiana University to obtain the J.D. degree, which he received with honors (1949). He worked one year as a law clerk to Judge H. Nathan Swaim in the U.S. Court of Appeals for the Seventh Circuit, after which he set up his law practice in Gary and has

Robert Anthony Lucas

been the senior partner in the firm of Lucas, Clifford, and Wildermuth since 1957.

While an undergraduate at Indiana University, Robert was active in the Sphinx Club, Blue Key, and Aeons. He was president of Delta Tau Delta social fraternity (1942–1943) and of the Student War Council. He was elected to the Beta Gamma Sigma (undergraduate scholastic honorary) and served as President of the Indiana Student Union (1942–1943). As a graduate student he was Associated Editor of the Indiana Law Journal, a member of Phi Delta Phi (legal fraternity) President (1947–1948), and was elected to the Order of the Coif.

Mr. Lucas's law experience was expanded with his appointment as Probate Commissioner (Judge) of the Lake Superior Court, where he served from January 1951 to November 1969. He also has been a Commissioner on Uniform State Laws from Indiana, member of the National Conference of Commissioners on Uniform State Laws (1966–). He holds membership in the Gary, Indiana, and American Bar Associations, American Judicature Society, and the Inter-American Bar Association, and is a Fellow of the American College of Probate Counsel.

In 1967 he was elected for a three-year term to the Board of Trustees of Indiana University, and in 1970 he was elected a member of the Board of the Indiana University Foundation. In 1971, he was appointed to the first Higher Education Commission of Indiana, was re-elected to the Board of the Indiana University Foundation in 1975, and is currently (in 1982) a member of that Board.

Among other activities, he has been the National Committeeman for the Young Democrats of Indiana (1949 to 1953) and has held memberships in the University and Country Clubs of Gary, the Indiana Society of Chicago, the Chicago Council on Foreign Relations, Elks, Optimists, and St. Barnabas Episcopal Church. He was President and Chairman of the Greater Gary Committee of "100." His Indiana connections continue through the Indiana University Alumni Association (President, 1973–74) and the Indiana University School of Law Alumni Association, of which he was President (1963). He also served as President of the IU Alumni Association of Gary (1960).

Mr. Lucas's business activities have encompassed a directorship and offices in numerous business entities including the Calumet Securities Corporation, Thermark Corporation (now a division of Avery International) N.A., the Bank of Indiana, and Money Management Corporation.

Charles Walter McCarty, 1891–1965
Trustee, 1945–1962

Charles Walter McCarty, newspaperman and civic leader, born April 30, 1898, was the son of John W. and Jennie (Denver) McCarty of Washington, Indiana, where his father was mayor for twenty years. Although he formally used C. Walter McCarty as his legal name, he was known widely as Mickey, or Mr. Mickey, and endeared himself to thousands during his professional career with his newspaper column "Mickey Says." He married Honore Harris on September 12, 1916, and they had one daughter, Sheila (Mrs. James Johnson, B.S. in Education, IUPUI, 1975).

Mickey entered Indiana University in 1911 as a journalism student and was graduated in 1914, having served as Editor of the *Daily Student,* Vice-President of the Indiana Union, Manager of the University Glee Club, and a founding member as well as the first President of the Press Club (which later became a chapter of Sigma Delta Chi, the national professional journalistic fraternity). The latter organization elected him posthumously to the Indiana Hall of Fame (1971). He also was a member of the Sigma Alpha Epsilon social fraternity. After he had retired as a Trustee, he received the Big Wheel award at the Gridiron banquet in 1964. This is an award for "the person outside the University who has done the most to spread the fame of Indiana University." In 1965, just ten days before he died, he was the recipient of the Distinguished Alumni award.

He began his career in journalism with a newspaper route for the *Washington Democrat* in Washington, Indiana, and later wrote high school notes for this same paper during his high-school days. He again assumed the role of "paper boy" in 1951

Charles Walter McCarty

by "selling" copies of *The News* to business and industry for contributions to the News Cheer Fund at Christmas Time.

Mickey worked briefly for the Associated Press but joined the *Indianapolis News* in 1914 as a police reporter; in 1926 he became City Editor; in 1932 Assistant Manager, during which time the paper won a Pulitzer Prize. He rose to Managing Editor in 1934 and served as President and General Manager of both the newspaper and its radio station, WIBC, from 1944–1948. When the *News* and *Star* merged into the Indianapolis Newspapers, Incorporated, Mickey became Editor of the *News*. In 1960 he was appointed Executive Editor.

Mickey was interested in the PAL Club, an organization sponsored by the Indianapolis Police Department to curb juvenile delinquency. The *News* sponsored professional football games yearly to raise money for this organization. His fifty-one years in the newspaper business brought him the "Newspaperman of the Year" award in 1965 from the Indianapolis Press Club. He also was a member of the Columbia and Athletic Clubs of Indianapolis and of St. Joan of Arc Catholic Church.

Mickey's long tenure as an Indiana University Trustee began in 1945, and the Board immediately appointed him to the Executive Committee of the Medical Center. He was a good friend to Indiana University and took personal interest in the welfare and the end product of the *Indiana Student*. He was unstinting in his use of the media to advance the status of Indiana University.

Well known as an outstanding toastmaster with a "keen wit and poetic tongue," he was the 1956 Master of Ceremonies of the Little 500 Variety Show. Although he had been ill for some time, he worked until the week before his death. Mr. McCarty was stricken during the afternoon of June 23, 1965, and died about 11 p.m. He is buried in Crown Hill Cemetery in Indianapolis.

Robert Franklin McCrea, 1915–1976
TRUSTEE, 1959–1965

Robert Franklin McCrea, lawyer and public official, son of Walter Pleasants and Alma (Webber) McCrea, was born in Logansport, Indiana, on July 30, 1915. His parents were Cass County farmers, as is his brother, Thomas. Robert graduated from Lucerne, Indiana, High School and entered Indiana University, receiving an A.B. in History (1937) and an LL.B. (1939). He lived in South Hall, the first dormitory for men, where he worked as a dining-room waiter for three years. Robert was active in Law School Moot Court trials and was a member of Phi Delta Phi (a legal honorary fraternity). Upon graduation, he entered the office of Alfred Evens where he remained until 1942, when he entered public service (January to June 1942) as the Deputy Prosecutor of Monroe County, the first of several public offices he held. At this time, Robert, a Lieutenant in the Army Officers Reserve, was called to Army service. By October 1945 when he was discharged, he attained the rank of Lieutenant Colonel. During his military service he spent from January 1943 to October 1945 in the South Pacific and Japan. In 1945 he established his own law office. From January 1946 through December 1951 Robert was the Prosecuting Attorney for Monroe County, an office to which he had been elected in November 1944 while still overseas; and finally, in January 1952, he became the Bloomington City Attorney.

Robert McCrea married Dorothy Ruth Smith (A.B. 1938) on October 14, 1939. They had three children: Barbara Ellen (Mrs. Jay Gordon Taylor, A.B. 1964, M.S. 1968; Mr. Taylor received a J.D. in 1967), David Smith (A.B. 1965, J.D. 1968; his wife, Elizabeth Statts, A.B. 1966, Ph.D. 1980), and Edward Franklin (A.B. Harvard, 1969; J.D., IU 1972). The law firm of McCrea and McCrea continues with David and Edward as the partners.

McCrea was a member of the Monroe County, Indiana State, and American Bar Associations; at various times he was President of the Indiana State Prosecutors' Association and

Robert Franklin McCrea

Secretary-Treasurer and later President of the Indiana University Law School Alumni Association. He served on the Indiana University School of Law Board of Visitors, the Indiana Bar Foundation, the Indiana State Bar Association Board of Managers, the Board of Directors of the Bloomington National Bank, the Advisory Board of the Hoosier Realty Corporation, and held a Supreme Court appointment to the Disciplinary Commission. He was a Republican, an elder of the First Presbyterian Church, and held membership in the American Legion, Lions, and Elks.

Robert McCrea died January 26, 1976, and is buried in Bloomington's Rose Hill Cemetery.

Frank Edward McKinney, Sr., 1904–1974
TRUSTEE, 1962–1969
President of the Board, 1965–1969

Frank Edward McKinney, Sr., banker, politician, and civic leader, was born Francis but preferred to use the name Frank. He was born on June 16, 1904, one of the three sons of Roscoe Anthony and Ann (Moss) McKinney. His entire life was spent on the south side of Indianapolis where Roscoe was a fire chief (1948–1951) and city councilman. Frank's father died in April 1965 at the age of eighty-five. Frank's paternal grandparents, George and Lydia McKinney, were born in Ireland. George was a soldier in the Civil War. Frank's maternal grandparents, Philip and Jacobena Moss were natives of Germany.

Frank attended Sacred Heart High School but had to quit after his second year. Since he wanted to be a banker and knew he had to get an education to do so, he began studying at night through the Indiana University Extension Division and the LaSalle Institute of Accounting. Later he received Honorary LL.D.'s from St. Francis College, Loretto, Pennsylvania, (1947) and from Indiana University (1970).

Margaret K. Warner, also a southside Indianapolis resident, the daughter of Frank and Katherine Warner, became Frank's wife on November 24, 1932. She was always considered a

Frank Edward McKinney, Sr.

partner and was a tremendous help to her husband in whatever he undertook. She was named Distinguished Citizen of the Year for 1965 by the 11th Indiana District of the American Legion, only the second woman so honored since the inception of the award in 1957. She died on September 13, 1972.

Frank and Margaret had four children: Claire Marie (Mrs. James C. Clark); Robert Warner (an Indiana University graduate, 1958) who died December 4, 1968; Frank E., Jr. (B.S. 1961, MBA 1962), who was a gold medal Olympic swimmer in 1960; and Ann Kathleen.

Frank began his banking career at age 15 as a bank messenger for the Meyer Kiser Bank in 1919 and by 1921 he was an Assistant Cashier of the Peoples State Bank in Indianapolis. The latter hired him as an auditor (1922). Later McKinney bought the Old Fidelity Trust Company and in January 1936 became its President, the youngest bank president in the country. He remained there until 1959 when he became Board Chairman of the American Fletcher National Bank.

Active in political and governmental affairs, McKinney held the following positions: Treasurer, Indianapolis Democratic City Committee (1928–1932); Treasurer, Marion County Democratic Centennial Committee (1932–1934); Treasurer, Marion County (1935–1939); Indiana sub-Treasurer, Democratic National Committee (1936); Vice-Chairman, Democratic National Finance Committee (1940); Chairman, Military Housing Commission, DOD, (1948–1949); Treasurer, Indiana Democratic State Centennial Committee (1948–1951); Chairman, Democratic National Committee (1951–1952); United States Delegate, International Monetary Conference held in Rome (1962), and Madrid (1964). In 1965, Frank turned down the offer of an appointment as Ambassador to Jamaica because of business and civic commitments. On May 9, 1968, he was approved as United States Ambassador to Spain, but during his hospitalization for a routine check-up in connection with this appointment, he discovered he had a heart problem and therefore asked to be relieved from this appointment.

During his business and professional life McKinney held many positions. He was Chairman of the Executive Committee of the Allegheny Corporation; Chairman of the Board and President of the Fidelity Bank and Trust Company (1935–1959); Chairman of the Board and Director of the American Fletcher National Bank and Trust Company (1959–1968); Chairman of the Board of American Fletcher Corporation (1969–1970); Chairman of the Board (1967–1971) and Chairman of the Executive Committee (1970–1972) of the American Fletcher Mortgage Investors. In 1972 he held directorships in the Indiana Bell Telephone Company, Indianapolis Power and Light Company, American Fletcher Corporation, American Fletcher National Bank and Trust Company, National Homes Corporation, American United Life Insurance Company, and the Shorewood Corporation. At various other times, he was a director of the Indiana Broadcasting Corporation, Knox Glass Company, New York Central Railroad, Philadelphia Suburban Water Company, United States Corrugated Fibre Box Company, James Whitcomb Riley Center, the professional Warrior football, and the Indians baseball teams. A friendship with Owen Bush put McKinney into baseball. At different times the two owned the old Louisville Colonels and the Indianapolis Indians. Later McKinney owned and was President of the Pittsburgh Pirates until 1950.

Frank had served in the Army as a Major (1942) and was discharged as a Colonel (1945). He served in the Advance Payment and Loan Branch Fiscal Division from 1942–1945 and was the Assistant Director of Contract Settlement in Washington, DC in 1945.

McKinney was appointed in 1962 to fill out the term of Indiana University Trustee McCarty who had resigned after twelve years of service. In 1963 he was appointed to succeed Willis Hickam, whose term had expired; and in 1966 McKinney was appointed for another full term, resigning in 1969 because of health problems. After he left the Board, he continued to serve Indiana University by accepting the Chairmanship of the IUPUI Board of Advisors.

In 1965 Frank was elected a Director of the Indiana University Foundation, was on the Board of the Indiana Law Enforcement Training Organization, was Treasurer of Civic Center Donors, Incorporated, and Director of the Hundred

Club of Indianapolis, Incorporated. He belonged to the following social clubs: Indianapolis Athletic (Director and President); Columbia, Highland Golf and Country; Meridian Hills Country; University in Indianapolis; Indiana Creek Country (Miami Beach, Florida); and Old Baldy (Saratoga, Wyoming).

McKinney was the first Indiana man to receive membership in the Sovereign Order of the Knights of Malta. He was a Director of the following civic organizations: Central Indiana Boy Scouts Council, Indiana Chamber of Commerce, Indianapolis Hospital Development Association, Indianapolis Civic Progress Association, Indianapolis United Fund, and a member of the American Legion Emerson Post #262. He also had served as a Trustee of St. Joseph College, Rensselaer, Indiana (1961–1971). On February 1, 1968 he was the recipient of the Horatio Alger Award.

Frank E. McKinney, Sr. died on January 9, 1974, and is buried in Calvary Cemetery.

Frank Edward McKinney, Jr., 1938–
Trustee, 1973–1976

Frank Edward McKinney, Jr., banker and civic leader, son of Frank Edward, Sr., and Margaret (Warner) McKinney (both deceased) was born in Indianapolis on November 3, 1938. He graduated from Cathedral High School (1957) before entering Indiana University in 1957, where he obtained a B.S. (1961) and an MBA (1962). He was a member of Sigma Alpha Epsilon social fraternity, Captain of the swimming team, and president of the Student Foundation Committee as an undergraduate. He won a bronze medal in the Olympics in 1956, and both a silver and a gold medal in 1960. He was elected to the International Swimming Hall of Fame in 1975.

Frank was a First Lieutenant in the United States Army Intelligence (1962–1964). When he returned from service, he was associated with the First National Bank of Chicago until December, 1967, when he joined the American Fletcher National Bank. He became President of the bank in 1972 and was elected Chairman of the Board in May 1973.

Frank Edward McKinney, Jr.

Frank married Katherine Berry (B.S. 1960) on August 18, 1962, and they had six children: Frank E. III, Katherine Marie, Margaret Leonard, Madeleine Warner, Robert Warner and Heather Claire.

McKinney holds professional membership in the Association of Reserve City Bankers, American Bankers Association (Member of Advisory Committee to The Treasury of the U.S.), American Institute of Banking, Association of Bank Holding Companies (member Task Force on Regional Banking Deregulation and its Executive Committee), Indiana Bankers Association, and the International Monetary Conference.

McKinney's other business affiliations include directorships on the Boards of: Allied Bank International (New York) (member of Executive Committee); American Fletcher Bank (Suisse) S.A.; Blue Shield of Indiana (member, Executive Committee, and Second Vice-President); Indiana Bell Telephone Company, Inc. (Audit Committee, Corporate Public Policy Advisory Committee); Indiana Power and Light Company (Executive Committee); Indianapolis Water Company and the American United Life Insurance Company.

Among his numerous current civic services, McKinney is on the Board of Directors for: Indiana State and Indianapolis Chambers of Commerce, International Institute of Sports, Science, and Medicine; Economic Club of Indianapolis; Indianapolis Museum of Art; Indiana State Symphony Society, Inc.; Executive Council on Foreign Diplomats; Corporate Community Council; and Indianapolis Convention and Visitors Bureau. He is on the Board of Governors for United Way of Greater Indianapolis, Inc., and the Indiana Newman Foundation; is a member of the Executive Council of Brebeuf Preparatory School, member of the James Whitcomb Riley Association, and is on the Advisory Board for the Natatorium, Track and Field Station at IUPUI.

McKinney holds memberships in The Indianapolis Athletic Club, Penrod Society, 702 Club, Indianapolis Press Club, Indiana Society of Chicago, American Legion, Newcomen Society of North America, Meridian Hills Country Club, Notre Dame Club of Indianapolis, "I" Men's Association of IU, and the "500" Festival Associates.

Frank was elected to the Board of Trustees in 1973 and served for one term.

He is a Democrat and attends St. Lukes Catholic Church.

Mary Rieman Maurer, 1895–
Trustee, 1945–1963
Vice-President of the Board, 1953–1963

Mary Rieman Maurer, of Marion County, the second woman to serve as Trustee of Indiana University, was born in Connersville, Indiana, April 5, 1895, the daughter of Charles A. Susan J. (Downs) Rieman. The family is of German descent. Mrs. Maurer's paternal grandparents came to America in 1868. They settled in Connersville and established a florist business which, after the passing of three-quarters of a century, was still conducted by the Rieman family. The maternal family ancestors (Downs) were of English-Scotch-Irish descent. They came to America in 1637 and settled first in New England. The Connersville branch of the family came to Indiana in the early part of the nineteenth century.

Mary Rieman attended the Connersville schools and was graduated from the Connersville High School in 1912. In September, 1912, she entered Indiana University and was graduated four years later with distinction (June, 1916) and was elected to Phi Beta Kappa. She also was an honorary member of Mortar Board, YMCA Cabinet, the Women's Council and the Arbutus Staff. After graduation she maintained an interest in Indiana University and became a member of the Executive Council of the IU Alumni Association (1931–34).

After her graduation she taught English in the Connersville High School, where she became head of the English department and assistant principal. She took postgraduate courses in English at the University of Wisconsin and Columbia University. In 1931 she served as president of the English Section of the Indiana State Teachers Association. Mary became a Regional Director of the National Association of Governing Boards of State Universities and Allied Institutions; she served

Mary Rieman Maurer

on various committees and was chairman of the Committee on Accreditation (1963). She was a charter member of the Connersville branch of the American Association of University Women and a member of Delta Kappa Gamma, an honorary for women teachers. She also was a member of D.A.R. For thirteen years she held the office of district president of Kappa Alpha Theta. She was grand vice-president and grand president of Tri Kappa. Mary also was very active in the IU Women's Club of Indianapolis.

Mary Rieman continued in her teaching position until 1934 when, on September 18, she married a classmate, William F. Maurer (A.B., with distinction, 1916 and also a Phi Beta Kappa). They moved to Indianapolis, where they lived until William died on October 23, 1974. He was buried in Crown Hill cemetery, Indianapolis. Mary moved back to Connersville because of her poor health, eventually entering of a nursing home there where she now resides (1982).

Mary was elected as a Trustee by the alumni in June 1945 and served consecutive terms ending in 1963. She chose not to run again in 1963 when she finished eighteen years of service as an Indiana University Trustee, the last ten as Vice-President. Following her election in 1945, she and her husband established The Maurer Award exemplified by a ruby "I" superimposed on a diamond "U," to be given to the oldest living alumna. It has been passed down to honored alumnae since then.

In 1964 Mary received the University's Distinguished Alumni Service Award.

Robert Henry Menke, 1919–
TRUSTEE, 1966–1972

Robert Henry Menke, a furniture manufacturer and civic leader, son of William E. and Clara (Moenkhaus) Menke, was born October 15, 1919, in Huntingburg, Indiana, was graduated from high school there, and entered Indiana University, from which he received his A.B. (1941) and A.M. (1953). He obtained the latter degree while a member of the

Robert Henry Menke

State Legislature, his graduate education having been delayed due to his service in the United States Air Force during World War II, in which he saw service in the Philippines and Japan.

In his senior year at Huntingburg High School, Robert received the Gimble Award (later called the Trester Award) as a player on the state finalist basketball team (1937). At Indiana, he again received the Gimble Award for athletic ability, scholarship, and sportsmanship. He was active in Phi Eta Sigma (freshman honorary), Board of Aeons, Blue Key, Sphinx Club, and was a member of Indiana University's 1940 NCAA Championship Basketball Team.

Shortly after returning from overseas military duty (1945), he was elected to membership on the Executive Council of the Indiana University Alumni Association and helped found *The Review,* an association publication for which he later wrote several articles. He taught government for a semester in 1953 after he received his A.M. degree. In 1960–61 Robert was president of the Alumni Association of the College of Arts and Sciences-Graduate School and later served as president of the Indiana University Alumni of DuBois County.

On August 12, 1944, Robert married Phyllis McMurtrie (A.B. 1972) of Huntingburg, and they had four children: Susan (Mrs. Reid Weir, A.B. 1970; Reid Weir, A.B. 1969); Karen (Mrs. Wayne Middendorf, A.B. DePauw 1970, DVM Purdue 1974); Robert, Jr. (B.S. Industrial Engineering, Millikin University); and David (M.D. 1981).

Robert Menke managed the Huntington Furniture Factory until 1952, when he established his own factory in Oakland and later added factories in Ferdinand, Huntingburg, and Lake Wales, Florida. He was elected to a term in the Indiana General Assembly in 1952–1953.

Long interested in various aspects of education, he was elected to the Oakland City College Board (1962), has been a Trustee of St. Benedict College, and was elected to a six-year term as a Trustee of Millikin University (1973). Acting on his belief that a trustee should know the community well, Robert Menke moved his family to Bloomington when elected to the IU Board of Trustees in 1966. He also believed a Trustee should not serve more than two terms and thus did not offer his name for re-election a third time. He had an avid interest in music and was a strong supporter of that school at IU.

In addition to his Trustee activities, Menke has served on the boards of numerous corporations. He is President of Natural Areas and Historical Trust, an organization which is helping to restore a city hall in Huntingburg and various structures in the community of New Harmony, Indiana. His business activities now include presidencies of the Ferdinand Furniture Company and Styline Corporation. He also is a tree farmer, operates craft and gift shops in New Harmony, and has apartment projects in Florida and Indiana.

Menke is a member of the "I" Men's Association, the Loyalty Group of the Varisty Club, Well House Society, Indiana Academy of Sciences, and is a three-time Sagamore of the Wabash. His civic activities have been wide-ranging. He has served as a delegate to President Eisenhower's National White House Safety Conference (1954), the representative for the mayors of Southern Indiana on the 1964 Trade Mission Tour to South America, and a 1969 Wilton Scholar (the representative of the United States at the Steying, Sussex, England Conference in April of that year). A leader in scouting, he has been a member of the Executive Board of the Buffalo Trace Council of Boy Scouts in Southern Indiana, President of the Forestry and Woodland Owners Association, Director and Vice-President of Indiana Nature Conservancy.

He has maintained an interest in IU and was appointed to the Arts and Sciences Board of Visitors concerned with establishing a summer institute for alumni in 1982. The latter year also brought his election to the Indiana Basketball Hall of Fame.

Jeanne Seidel Miller, 1925–

Trustee, 1971–1974

Jeanne Seidel Miller, attorney, daughter of Carl F. and Adah K. (Gumpper) Seidel, was born in Fort Wayne on October 4, 1925. She attended South Side High School in Fort Wayne

Jeanne Seidel Miller

and entered Indiana University where she obtained an A.B. in Government (1946) and a J.D. (1948).

At Indiana, Jeanne was a member of Kappa Alpha Theta social sorority, the Article Editor of the Indiana Law Journal, a member of the Indiana University Debate Team, Board of Standards, Order of the Coif, Alpha Lambda Delta (freshman scholarship society), and Phi Beta Kappa. She won the Phi Delta Phi scholarship cup in 1948, the first woman to do so.

On September 9, 1947, Jeanne married Mickey M. Miller (J.D. 1948) and they had three children: Ward W. (A.B. 1971, Dartmouth; J.D., 1974, IU); Carl Michael (A.B. 1973, J.D. 1976); Marjorie A. (A.B. 1976). Jeanne has practiced law in New Haven since 1951.

At the time Governor Whitcomb appointed Mrs. Miller to the Indiana University Board of Trustees, she was President of the East Allen County School Board. She also had been President of the Allen County School Reorganization Committee. Jeanne has been active in both the Indiana and American Bar Associations, having been a Director of the Indiana Lawyers Commission, Chairman of the Indiana State Bar Association's Judicial Improvement Committee, and a member of its Board of Managers. She also has been a Director of the American Judicature Society and a member of the Indiana Supreme Court Disciplinary Commission.

In 1977 she won the third Ralph E. Broyles Award, given annually for unique and significant contributions to Indiana University at Fort Wayne.

William Hall Mohr, 1956–
Student Trustee, 1979–1981

William Hall Mohr, (A.B. 1979, senior-year Indiana University Medical School student) son of George William (B.S. Business 1942) and Joan (Goldsmith) (IU 1941–43, A.B. Butler 1945), was born August 29, 1956, in Kokomo, where he attended school through high school. Bill's grandfather taught at the Indianapolis Law School. Bill's older brother graduated from

William Hall Mohr

Indiana University Law School (LL.B. 1975), and his younger brother entered Indiana University in the fall of 1980.

During his undergraduate days at Indiana University, Mohr was very active in student affairs. He was a member of the Student Foundation (1977–79), Treasurer (1977–78) and then President (1978–79) of the Student Athletic Board, and Vice-President of the Board of Aeons (1978–79). In broader university activities, Bill served as the student representative on the University Athletic Committee (1978–79) and the Search and Screen Committee for a new Athletic Director (1978); he was an ex-officio member of the Varsity Club Board of Directors (1978–79), a member of the Student Advisory Committee for the Dean of Student Services (1978–79), and a member of the Board of Trustee's Student Committee to Evaluate the Office of the President (1978).

Bill was active in intramural sports, playing football and volleyball, and participating in track. However, he still found time to serve on many committees for his social fraternity, Phi Kappa Psi, for which he also was a fraternity educator.

Many academic honors and scholarships came to Mohr, among which were memberships in Phi Beta Kappa, Blue Key, Mortar Board, Phi Eta Sigma, and Alpha Lamda Delta. He received one of the five Elvis J. Starr awards (1979) given to Bloomington students, the local Matthew Winters Award (1978, 1979), and was the local recipient of the national Solon E. Summerfield Award (1978) from Phi Kappa Psi.

During the summers Bill worked some sixty to seventy hours per week as a truck driver for an asphalt paving company owned by his family.

Bill is a Protestant and a Republican. Governor Bowen appointed him for a two-year term on July 1, 1979, from an original field of thirty-nine applicants. He replaced retiring Student Trustee Jim Wolfe.

Elizabeth Blumberg Polley, 1910–
Trustee, 1980–

Elizabeth Blumberg Polley, businesswoman, artist, and supporter of the arts, daughter of Monta Wells and Charley D. Foster, was born in Columbus, Indiana, on July 16, 1910. She attended local secondary schools, completed her freshman year at IU-Bloomington, and then entered the Herron Art School for two years (1928–30), receiving a B.S. (1931) from Indiana University. She later obtained an M.S. (1938) and an Ed.D. (1952) from Indiana University. While at the University she was elected to Alpha Psi Omega, (dramatic's honorary), and Chi Omega social sorority.

Elizabeth, better known as "Betty," married Ben Blumberg on November 5, 1965 (deceased 1971) and has four stepchildren by that marriage: Morris, Rachel (Mrs. Norman Haskell), Theresa (Mrs. Stanley Hoffman), and Gretchen (Mrs. Victor Tatelman). On April 24, 1982, she married Dr. Howard F. Polley of the Mayo Clinic and has three stepchildren through that marriage: William Polley, Alice (Mrs. Fred Breimyer), and Mary Ann (Mrs. Dale McCoy).

After receiving her B.S., Betty was an art instructor at Indiana Central College (1931–33), an art supervisor (1934–36) at Crown Point, Indiana, and at Rushville, Indiana (1936–37). She then moved to Manual Training High School in Indianapolis, where she was Chairman of the Art Department (1937–48). Meanwhile Betty also was an art instructor in the evening division of Butler University (1939–43) and a part-time reporter and feature writer for the *Indianapolis News* (1939–43). While working on her Ed.D. degree, Betty was a graduate assistant (1948–50). She then became Associate Professor of Art at Indiana State University (1950–65).

Upon the death of her husband, Betty took over as Vice-President of the 624 Corporation and the Progress Building Corporation, and became the owner of Blumberg Farms. She assumed the Chairmanship of the Board of Acorn Studios, Inc. (1975–); is a Director of Indiana Blue Cross (1976–) and a member of its Executive Committee (1978–); a member of the Indiana Committee for the Humanities Board (1978,

Elizabeth Blumberg Polley

Vice-President 1982-) and the Indiana Public Broadcasting Society (1980-).

Polley has been active in many local and national civic and political organizations. Among those she has served are: the American Red Cross, Wabash Valley Chapter (Chairman, 1968; Executive Committee, 1969-75, 1977-80); Katherine Hamilton Mental Health Center (Secretary, Board of Directors, 1968-69); Swope Art Gallery; Terre Haute Boys Club (Director, 1971-82); Terre Haute Regional Hospital (Trustee, 1975-81; Chairman, 1980-81); Vigo County Fair Board (1977-82); Terre Haute Symphony (Director, 1972-82; Vice-President, 1974-78); Women's Service League of Union Hospital (1974-); U.S. Bond Sales (Indiana Woman's Chairman, 1968-); Hoosier Salon Patrons Association (Director, 1971-77); Indiana Orchestra Association (Director, 1974-78); Indiana Nature Conservancy (Director, 1977-81; Life Trustee 81-); Commission of Aged and Aging (Committee, 1975-80); St. Mary-of-the-Woods College (Board of Associates, 1979-81); Indiana University (Elected Trustee, 1980-).

Betty holds life memberships in Indiana University Friends of Music (Director, 1976-), Indiana University Alumni Association and the Indianapolis Museum of Art; memberships in Friends of Lilly Library, Theatre Circle, Woodburn Guild, Friends of Art (Director 1979-), The Well House Society, Indiana Press Club, Indiana Artists Club (1940-; Secretary, 1942-46), National Education Association (1931-65), American Pen Women (1954-), American Association of University Professors (1950-65), Women's Department Club of Terre Haute (Director, 1969), Business and Professional Women's Club (President, 1962; State Chairman International Relations, three-year term; District Director 1969), Federation of Jewish Women (Director, 1969; 1974-76; President, 1973-74), National Arts Club (1942-), Metropolitan Opera National Council (1969-), and the American Angus Association.

Betty also has served as a delegate from the United States to the International Congress of Business and Professional Women's Clubs in Paris (1936) and has been involved in numerous Republican workshops and political Caucus activities. She received the medal for distinguished service given by

Indiana University's Indiana Memorial Union (1949), was named Women of the Year (1971) by Terre Haute Business and Professional Women's Club, won the J. I. Holcomb Water Color Prize (1936) and the Louis Schwitzer Oil Painting Prize (1937), received a twenty-five-year plaque for organizing and directing the first Indiana University European tour for university credit (1950–1975), and was named Honorary Speaker of the Indiana House of Representatives (1978).

Earl Burton Pulse, 1908–1959
Trustee, 1955–1959

Earl Burton Pulse, Columbus businessman, son of Bert and Alta C. (Joslin) Pulse, was born on March 25, 1908, in Columbus, Indiana. His mother died February 26, 1956, and his father in April 1957. Earl graduated from Columbus High School in 1926 and received a B.S. in Commerce and Finance (1930) from Indiana University's Business School, where he was a member of Delta Chi social fraternity and Alpha Kappa Psi (business honorary). He later served as President of the Delta Chi State Alumni Association (President of IU Chapter, 1929–1930). As an Indiana University freshman, Earl played basketball and baseball and participated in intramural sports.

On June 6, 1937, Pulse married Hazel Simmons of Columbus, Indiana. They had two children: Mary Ann Pulse McCray (A.B. 1960) and Earl B. Jr. (B.S. 1962, LL.B. 1965), both of whom were enrolled at Indiana University when their father died on June 8, 1959.

Shortly after his marriage, Earl joined the Union Starch and Refining Company (October 1937), rising through the administrative ranks from Secretary to Director, Vice-President, Treasurer, and finally President in 1953, which office he held until his death in 1959. Additionally, he held an appointment as an Associate Faculty member in the Indiana University School of Business for the 1954–55 school year, during which he lectured upperclassmen and assisted in the School's placement program. He was instrumental in setting up the Exec-

Earl Burton Pulse

utive Development summertime program for promising businessmen of the state.

Pulse was a Trustee of the North Christian Church in Columbus and a Republican. He held memberships in the Blue Lodge, Scottish Rite, and York Rite of the Masonic Order. In 1953 he served as Ninth District Chairman of the Nationwide American-Korean Foundation campaign to raise funds for widows and orphans in Korea. He had served as President of the Columbus Chamber of Commerce and Kiwanis; elected to the Columbus City Council, he served them faithfully; and in 1954 he was Chairman of the Indiana Study Commission on Intergovernmental Relations. Prior to being appointed Trustee of Indiana University in 1955, Earl held directorships in the Christian Foundation and Christian Theological Seminary at Indianapolis and the Corn Industries Research Foundation in New York. He was reappointed as an IU Trustee in 1958 but died before he finished his second term.

Earl also was a Director of the American United Life Insurance Company of Indianapolis and had memberships in the Columbia and Athletic Clubs of Indianapolis as well as the Athletic Club and the Merchants' Exchange of St. Louis, Missouri.

Pulse had suffered a severe heart attack in July 1957 from which he had recovered completely and had returned to his many business and civic activities. On June 2, 1959, he had the attack which resulted in his death just one week later on June 8 at Bartholomew County Hospital. Services were held in North Christian Church, of which he was an elder. He is buried in Garland Brook Cemetery in Columbus, Indiana.

John Stewart Riley, 1899-1965
TRUSTEE, 1957-1963

John Stewart Riley (he preferred to use Stewart as his given name), newspaper executive, the son of John V. (former publisher of the *Rockford Morning Star* in his native city of Rockford, Illinois) and Lenore (Hooker) Riley, was born in Rockford, Illinois, on February 4, 1899. He attended schools

John Stewart Riley

in Rockford until he graduated from Rockford High School in 1916. He obtained his B.A. from Hamilton College (Clinton, New York, 1920), where he was a member of Delta Kappa Epsilon social fraternity and a member of the college track team. He began his newspaper career in 1920 in the advertising department of the Davenport (Iowa) *Daily Times*. He joined the *Rockford Morning Star* in 1923, becoming its advertising director, and, in 1927, he inherited his father's half-interest in Rockford Newspapers, Incorporated, which he sold (1930) when the Rockford papers were merged.

He engaged in commercial printing for the next twelve years. In addition, he taught at Rockford High School (1932 and 1933), and served as a trustee of Rockford College from 1934 to 1940, when he left Rockford.

Stewart was a graduate student at the University of Wisconsin and for three quarters at the University of Chicago (1940–1942) and then moved to Bedford and purchased the *Times* and *Mail,* merging them into the *Times Mail.* Thus, he never finished the M.A. which he had been pursuing at the University of Chicago. He also served six months in the Army during World War I. He expanded his newspaper holdings with the purchases of the Herrin (Illinois) *Daily Journal* and the Murphysboro (Illinois) *Independent* in 1944 and 1945, respectively, which he published until he sold them in 1947, at which time he established the *Bloomington Daily-Herald*. He then purchased the controlling interest in the *World Telephone* which was merged with the *Bloomington Daily Herald* in 1950 to become the *Herald-Telephone* with Riley as publisher.

Stewart married Dagmar Karlson of Chicago, Illinois, on December 18, 1943. They had one daughter, Katherine Anne, who was an Indiana University junior in 1965 when her father died. On November 18, 1966, Katherine, then a senior, met a tragic end in an automobile accident.

Stewart was the first publisher in the United States to build a new plant following World War II, and the *Times Mail* launched its operations in this new plant (1947). In 1961 he moved the *Herald-Telephone* into a new building he had built for it in Bloomington.

Although not a native Hoosier, Stewart loved his adopted

state and, as a publisher of two leading southern Indiana newspapers, did outstanding service for that area. Likewise, although he was not an Indiana University alumnus and did keep close ties to his alma mater, Hamilton College, he was a strong supporter of Indiana University. When he became an Indiana University Trustee in 1957, he already had five years experience as a Trustee for Rockford College. From the time he was appointed in 1957, he made it a point "to do his homework" and to take on what he considered the responsibilities of a Trustee. He also served as an Indiana University Foundation board member.

Stewart was concerned about the image of the University and wrote positive editorials to help build a good one, and he was interested in ways to develop alumni contributions and other sources for Indiana University funding. His interest and enthusiasm were so contagious that the employees of the *Herald-Telephone*, in looking for a way to honor Mr. and Mrs. Riley, established the Stewart and Dagmar Riley yearly journalism scholarship in 1958. Stewart's wife, Dagmar, was closely associated with him in the newspaper business, both in Bedford and Bloomington. She was the Executive Vice-President of the latter paper, and after Stewart's death she was named President and Treasurer of Bloomington Newspapers, Incorporated, as well as publisher of the *Daily Herald-Telephone*. She assumed the same positions with the *Bedford Times-Mail*.

When his term as Trustee expired in 1963, Stewart continued to maintain both his interest in and help to Indiana University. He used his newspaper columns and his personal contacts in every way possible to assist the University.

Mrs. Riley moved to Bloomington in 1968 and in January, 1968, the Trustees created the J. Stewart Riley Professorship of Journalism, which was made possible by Mrs. Riley's gift to the Indiana University Foundation in memory of her husband.

Stewart had been a member of the Rockford University Club Board for six years and a member of the Board of Governors of Rockford City Club while he resided in Rockford. The Community Chest (later the United Way) was among his major civic interests. Before moving to Bedford he was President of the Rockford Community Chest, and in Bedford he served on the Board of the Bedford Community Chest three different times.

In his professional field, Riley was a member (1951-1957), Chairman of the Board of Directors (1959) and President (1956) of the 600-member Inland Press Association. He joined the American Society of Newspaper Editors in 1957 and was a member of the Hoosier State and International Press Associations. Stewart was the founder and first President of Southern Indiana, Incorporated (1952)—a regional Chamber of Commerce formed to promote conservation, tourism, and the establishment of new industry in southern Indiana. The Civic Newcomers, Incorporated, a nationwide service welcoming new people to a community, was originated by Stewart and he installed such a unit in Bloomington when he launched the *Daily Herald.*

He was not a complacent man; he held strong opinions on subjects in which he was interested and put all his energy and effort into accomplishing goals in which be believed. World travel was more than a hobby, and his observations of world conditions became the subject of countless editorials in his newspapers.

Stewart's other active interests were in the Kiwanis, Elks, Masonic Lodge, Crane Area Council of the Navy League, and the First United Presbyterian Church in Bedford.

Riley had long been troubled by emphysema and finally had to have two operations in February and March, 1965, while in Arizona. A third operation followed in May after he returned to Indiana. Stewart died on June 6, 1965, at Long Hospital in Indianapolis. He was buried in Cresthaven Memory Garden in Bedford.

Donald Aquilla Rogers, 1901-1969
Trustee, 1963-1966

Donald Aquilla Rogers, attorney and Superior Court Judge, was born February 17, 1901, in Evansville, Indiana, the third son of Lon D. and Florence (Barnhill) Rogers. Donald's par-

Donald Aquilla Rogers

ents came from old-stock Monroe County families; and, although at the time of Donald's birth they were temporarily in Evansville, they returned to Monroe County four years later. Donald graduated from Bloomington High School in 1919 and received his LL.B. (1927) from Indiana University. While still a student in law school, he worked as the deputy county clerk and before he graduated was elected deputy prosecuting attorney and served for one term after graduation. In 1932 he was elected Judge of the Monroe/Owen Circuit Court. When the state legislature created a new circuit for Owen County in 1938, Donald was re-elected as Judge for the Monroe Circuit Court. Later, in 1965, when the Monroe County Superior Court was established, he was appointed to that post and then was elected for a four-year term in 1966.

Donald Rogers married Laura Marie Woolery (B.A. 1923) on August 20, 1924, and they had three children: Barbara Marie (Mrs. John H. Houseworth, A.B. 1946; Mr. Houseworth, M.D. 1947), John Willliam (B.S. in Business 1950), and Leon David (A.B. 1950, J.D. 1955; his wife, Virginia, M.S. in Education 1950). Donald's father, Lon D. Rogers, graduated in 1878; his brother Leon B. (A.B. 1912) and Marion C. (A.B. 1922) and all four of his grandchildren also have graduated from Indiana University.

Donald enlisted in the Army (military government, 1943) as a Captain and was promoted to Major in 1945. He served overseas in Africa, Italy, and Austria. After the war, he opened his law office in Bloomington in 1946, and his son, State Senator David Rogers, went into joint practice with his father in 1956. When J. Stewart Riley's term as Trustee expired in June 1963, Donald was appointed to replace him. He was reappointed for another three-year term in 1966. However, in December of that year he submitted his resignation to Governor Branigin because of his increased workload in the court and because he wanted to avoid any possible conflict of interest that might arise should a case involving the University come before his court.

Judge Rogers was very active in community as well as university affairs. He was a member of the Indiana Bar Association, Order of the Coif, Phi Delta Phi, Phi Delta Theta, Redman's Lodge, Knights of Pythias, Masonic Lodge, and American Legion. He served on the Board of Governors of the American Law Institute, was past President of the Bloomington Kiwanis and of the White River Council of the Boy Scouts, and past County Chairman of the Democratic party.

He was a member of the First Christian Church, past Board Chairman of the Indiana School of Religion, and held directorships for the Monroe County State Bank and the Workingmen's Savings and Loan Association.

Judge Rogers's brother, Marion, survived him, but his brother, Leon, died in 1955. Judge Rogers died October 19, 1969, and is buried in Bloomington's Rose Hill Cemetery.

Leslie Curtis Shively, 1954–

STUDENT TRUSTEE, January 1976– June 1977

Leslie Curtis Shively, student, accounting major, son of Ronald R. and Violet (Schneider) Shively, was born May 22, 1954, in Evansville, Indiana, where he attended public schools. He was graduated in 1972 and received the Chamber of Commerce Distinguished High School Graduate Award. He attended Indiana University, where he earned a B.S. (1976), an MBA (1980), and a J.D. (1980).

Shively was the first Student Trustee appointed by Governor Bowen. Since his appointment occurred at the end of the first semester of the school year, his tenure was for a year and one-half instead of the two-year term proposed for Student Trustees.

Leslie was a member of Phi Gamma Delta social fraternity, Phi Eta Sigma scholastic honorary, Blue Key, Phi Delta Phi legal fraternity, and a past president of the Interfraternity Council (1974–75). He was a member of the Health Center Student Advisory Board, the Student Foundation, the Student Association Senate, and was the recipient of the Elvis J. Stahr Award (1976). He was a founder and member of the Board of Directors of the Methodist Temple Inner City Camp in Evansville, Indiana. He spent two summers (1974, 1975) as an

Leslie Curtis Shively

intern to Mayor Russell G. Lloyd and with the Department of Metropolitan Development in Evansville, Indiana, and as an assistant to the Controller's Office of the American Dairy Company in Evansville.

Leslie married Lourdes C. Pollard on September 13, 1980, and they live in Evansville, where Leslie is associated with the law firm of Johnson, Carroll, and Griffith.

Shively has continued his interest in and association with Indiana University in various capacities. He was a member of the School of Business Alumni Advisory Board (1981–84) and President of the Vanderburgh County IU Alumni Association (1980).

He has been a member of the Indiana and Evansville Bar Associations since 1980. He also is on the Board of Directors of the Conrad Baker Foundation (1980–84) and has been active in the Southwestern Indiana United Way Fund Drive, and served on the Republican Finance Committee (1980) and as a Republican Precinct Committeeman (1982).

Richard Burkett Stoner, 1920—
Trustee, 1972–
President of the Board, 1980–

Richard Burkett Stoner, Industrialist and civic leader, son of Edward N. and Florence (Burkett) Stoner was born May 15, 1920, in Ladoga, Indiana. He graduated from Tipton High School in 1937 and entered Indiana University, where he obtained a B.S. (1941) and was President of his class. He then went on to Harvard Law School, obtaining the J.D. in 1947.

While at Indiana, Richard, better known as Dick was President of the Union Board and of his senior class, a member of Sigma Nu social fraternity (and served as President), Beta Gamma Sigma honorary society in commerce, and Blue Key.

He married Virginia B. Austin on February 22, 1942, and they had six children: Pamela T. (Mrs. Michael Burt, A.B. 1962), Richard B., Jr., Benjamin A., Janet E. (Mrs. Robert Abrams, M.S. Art Education 1976), Rebecca Lee (Mrs. Randal Kirts, 1972–75), and Joanne J. Stoner.

Richard Burkett Stoner

Since his graduation in 1947, Stoner has been with the Cummins Engine Company in various administrative and executive positions. He currently (1982) is the Vice-Chairman of the Board.

During World War II he served as a Captain in the Army Finance Department. He has long had an interest in education and Governor Branigin named Stoner to the Chairmanship of a twenty-nine member Post-High School Public Education Commission (1968) charged with devising a twenty-year master plan for Indiana education. In 1971 he was named the Chairman of the first annual Indiana University School of Business Development Fund Drive. The year before he had been chosen as one of the first five members of a newly created Academy of Alumni Fellows of the Business School.

Politically active, he has been on the Indiana Democratic State Central Committee since the early 1950s, has been a Democratic National Committeeman from Indiana since 1966, and has been an Indiana delegate to every Democratic National Convention since 1956.

Stoner's other activities include: President of the Indiana Forum, Incorporated (1970); Trustee and Past President of the Christian Theological Seminary (Indianapolis); Director, American Fletcher National Bank and Trust Company and American Fletcher Corporation (1969–); Director, Indiana State Chamber of Commerce (1969–); Area Four President, East Central Region Boy Scouts (1972–74); Director, Public Service Company of Indiana (1974–); Director, American United Life Insurance Company, Indianapolis (1976–); member of Indiana Academy. He is also a member of the Disciples of Christ Church and a past-member of the General Board and is Vice-President-at-large of the National Council of Churches of Christ in the USA (1961–73).

He was first appointed a Trustee of Indiana University in 1972 and has thrice been reappointed. He became President of the Board of Trustees in 1980, succeeding Danny Danielson.

Ray Cecil Thomas, 1898–1971
TRUSTEE, 1952–1967
Vice-President of the Board, 1962–1967

Ray Cecil Thomas, Gary lawyer and businessman, was born in Alexandria, Indiana, on December 11, 1898, the son of Berton and Birdie (Painter) Thomas.

He lived in Alexandria, Indiana, until shortly after he graduated from high school in 1917. Then he moved to Los Angeles, his home until the fall of 1918, when he returned to Indiana to enter Indiana University. Ray received the A.B. (1922) and the LL.B. (1924). He moved to Miami, Florida, where he lived until the fall of 1926. On February 20, 1926, he married Josephine Kelly (A.B. 1922) of Mt. Vernon, Indiana, and later that year they took up residence in Gary, Indiana, where they remained until Ray's death on August 23, 1971. They had one son, Joseph, born February 20, 1929. He received a B.S. degree (1951) from Indiana University's School of Business. After receiving his LL.B. from Harvard, (1954) he joined his father, Ray, as a law partner in Gary.

Ray C. Thomas served as a private in World War I and served again in World War II, for over three years, in the Judge Advocate General's Corps of the Army, finally attaining the rank of Colonel. He was awarded the Bronze Star and Army Commendation Ribbon and was decorated by the French government with the *Medaille de la Reconnaissance Francaise.*

As a student, Ray was very active. A charter member of the Indiana chapter of Acacia, for which he later served as a national councilor from 1946–1950, he was given the national Acacia Award of Merit (1965) for his long and continued support of the organization. At Indiana University he was a member of Gamma Eta Gamma legal fraternity, the Garrick Club, the "I" Men's Association, and he served as President of the Scabbard and Blade (military fraternity). He also was a member of the Arbutus Staff. Thomases have been known on the Indiana University Campus since 1850, and from among the forty-four members of Mr. and Mrs. Thomas's families at

Ray Cecil Thomas

least one has usually been in attendance on the Bloomington Campus at any given time.

Ray's wide-ranging interest in University activities continued during his professional life. He served as national Vice-President of the Indiana University Alumni Association, President of the Lake County Indiana University Club, Secretary of the Indiana University Alumni Advisory Committee, organizer and trustee of four student loan foundations. He was elected by the Indiana University Alumni (1952) as trustee to replace Judge Ora L. Wildermuth, who had served for twenty-seven years on the Board. Ray C. Thomas served for fifteen consecutive years, being re-elected every three years until he retired in 1967 because of health problems.

His Gary activities included membership in the American Legion Post, the Masonic Lodge, the Kiwanis, and the Country Club. He was a trustee of the First Presbyterian Church, a Director of the YMCA, director of the Men's Division of the Red Cross Drive in 1946, and was on the board of directors of the Chamber of Commerce. He was president of the Indiana Reserve Officers Association, and a member of the Republican Party. Ray C. Thomas was actively involved in obtaining the land for the Indiana University Gary Campus from the City of Gary.

Late in 1967, after Ray's hospitalization and recovery from a heart attack, Mr. and Mrs. Thomas spent five months visiting various areas of the South Pacific, stopping in Hawaii for several weeks en route home. While there, he made it a point to visit Ernie Pyle's grave, since they had been classmates at Indiana University, and he informed President Stahr that the grave was well taken care of and supplied with red and white flowers by the Indiana University Alumni in Hawaii.

Ray C. Thomas died at Methodist Hospital in Gary and is buried in Calumet Park Cemetery.

John Daniel Widaman II, 1917–1972
Trustee 1970–1972

John Daniel Widaman II, attorney, son of Allan S. and Florence (Irvine) Widaman was born in Warsaw, Indiana, on April 30, 1917. He attended school in Warsaw through high school and then entered Indiana University, where he obtained an A.B. (1939) and an LL.B. (1942). John was a member of Beta Theta Pi and Vice-President of the Indiana Law Club. He received varsity football letters in 1937 and 1938.

On June 20, 1941, John married Marjorie Heidenreich (B.S. 1941), and they had four children: Kathryn (Mrs. Kathryn Kuhn), John D. Widaman III (B.S. 1971, J.D. 1974), Krista (Mrs. Joseph Koors, Associated Degree in Business 1975), and Karen Widaman (B.S. 1978).

After graduating from Indiana University, John served as an FBI agent until he joined the United States Navy during World War II. He held the rank of Lieutenant and served in the European and African Theaters.

Returning from the Navy, he set up his law practice in Warsaw. His primary practice was devoted to trial cases, and he became a Fellow by invitation of the American College of Trial Lawyers. His other professional memberships were the American and Indiana State Bar Associations, and he was a past member of the Board of Managers of the latter organization. In addition to his professional memberships, he also belonged to the Rotary Club, Elks, Masons, Consistory, Shrine, and was a President of the Warsaw Chamber of Commerce. He was a Republican and belonged to the First Presbyterian Church in Warsaw. John was appointed to the Indiana University Board of Trustees on August 20, 1970, to fill out the term of Judge Jesse Eschbach, who had resigned for business reasons. At the expiration of this term he was reappointed by Governor Whitcomb for a full term starting in July 1971.

Mr. and Mrs. Widaman were traveling in the Far East on an official trip with a group visiting a number of Indiana University Educational Projects in the area when they were killed in a plane accident en route from Bangkok to Hong Kong.

John Daniel Widaman II

Howard Samuel Wilcox, 1920–
TRUSTEE, 1963–1966

Howard Samuel (Howdy) Wilcox, newspaperman and currently (1982) Indianapolis Public Relations Counselor, the son of Howard Samuel and Catherine (Dugan) Wilcox was born February 3, 1920, in Indianapolis. He graduated from Shortridge High School there and attended Indiana University in Bloomington (A.B. 1942). He later attended the United States Army Command and General Staff College, graduating with honors (1961), and received the Commandant's Award for Distinguished Writing.

He married Betty Tuck on June 20, 1942, and they had four sons: Howard S., Jr., (B.S. 1966, MBA 1967, JD 1971, he also attended West Point); Donald DuVall, David Warren, and Scott Robert (David and Scott also attended Indiana University).

At Indiana University, "Howdy" was student assistant of the News Bureau, later editor of the *Indiana Daily Student,* a member of Sigma Delta Chi (professional journalism fraternity, which presented him with the Big Wheel Award in 1961), Pershing Rifles, Scabbard and Blade, and Sphinx Club. He served as President of both Skull and Cresent and the Alpha Tau Omega social fraternity. He won the Sigma Delta Chi Journalism and Mary K. Burnett Senior Scholarships for men.

Commissioned a Second Lieutenant in the University's ROTC, he spent two years after graduation at the infantry school in Fort Benning, Georgia, from which he was assigned to the European command as an Infantry Company Commander. Later, as a Battalion Commander, he received the Silver Star, Bronze Star with Oak Leaf Cluster, and Purple Heart. On two occasions his unit received presidential citations. He reached the rank of Lieutenant Colonel before being discharged and was one of eighteen American officers to receive the British Military Cross from Field Marshall Montgomery. He continued his military interests in reserve units after his return from Europe. He became Commanding General of the Indiana 38th Infantry Division in 1963, and as of 1976 he was Assistant Commanding General for Reserve Af-

Howard Samuel Wilcox

fairs of the Army's Forces Command. He retired from the U.S. Army in August 1976, with the rank of Major General and was awarded the Army's Legion of Merit. President Nixon named Howdy to the Board of Visitors, U.S. Academy at West Point (1974), and he served as Chairman of the Board in 1976.

Howard Wilcox was in the advertising business in Indianapolis from 1946–1948. During this time he taught advertising for two years at the Indiana University Extension Center in Indianapolis. In 1948, he was elected President of the Indiana Chapter of the National Industrial Advertising Association.

Howdy became Executive Director of the Indiana University Foundation (July 1949), from which he resigned on August 31, 1952. During his three-year incumbency, he organized the Student Foundation Committee and originated the "Little 500" bicycle race. The latter was an application of his heritage as the son of Howdy Wilcox, the winner of the 1919 "big" 500 Indianapolis Memorial Day Race. His interest in Indiana University and the Foundation remained even though he left in 1952 to become associated with the *Indianapolis Star* and the *Indianapolis News* as Director of Personnel and Public Relations for these two newspapers. He became the General Manager of the *Arizona Republic* and *Phoenix Gazette* (1963), returning to Indianapolis (1966) to set up the public relations counseling firm which bears his name. In July of that year the University contracted with this firm to assist in the development of the Indianapolis campus, and the firm continues (1982) to be associated with Indiana University in a broad public relations role.

Wilcox was elected to the Indiana University Board of Trustees in 1963. He completed his full term although he had taken a job in Arizona.

Wilcox married Joyce Dunford Lowe of Warsaw, Indiana, on July 11, 1975.

He belongs to the Masons, Consistory (receiving the thirty-three degree in September 1982), and the Shrine.

Howdy currently (1982) is a Trustee of Freedoms Foundation at Valley Forge, Pa., and President of Public TV Station

WFYI (Channel 20 in Indianapolis). He holds directorships in: the Indiana State Chamber of Commerce (also member of the Executive Committee), Indianapolis Chamber of Commerce, IU Foundation (also member of Executive Committee), General Employment Enterprises, Inc., in Chicago (also member of Audit Committee and Chairman of Compensation Committee), Wabash International Corp (Indianapolis), The Unified Companies (Investment Funds, Indianapolis, also member of Executive Committee), Indianapolis Bar Foundation, Indiana Science Education Fund, Inc., and the Alpha Tau Omega Foundation.

Ora Leonard Wildermuth, 1882–1964

TRUSTEE, 1925–1952

Vice-President of the Board, 1936–1938

President of the Board, 1938–1950

Ora Leonard Wildermuth, lawyer of Lake County, was born on his father's farm near Star City, Pulaski County, Indiana, on October 15, 1882, son of Elias and Olive (Herrick) Wildermuth. The Wildermuth family had come from Germany to America in 1752 and settled in Pennsylvania near Valley Forge. One of the forebears of Ora Wildermuth was a soldier of the Revolution. Ora's grandfather moved to Ohio, staying briefly in Fairfield County of that state, and then drove west to settle in Pulaski County, Indiana, where Ora's father was born, reared, married, and made his home.

Ora went to the graded district school, of which he had interesting memories, and later to Star City High School, about three miles from the home farm. He was a member of the first high school class in that township. When it developed that he would be the only senior in his last year in high school, the township trustee refused to employ an extra teacher for one student, and the future judge was forced to go to Winamac, the county seat ten miles distant, to complete his course.

He was graduated from the Winamac High School in 1901, and in the Fall of 1902 entered the School of Law at Indiana University. At that time, law was a three-year course, but Ora

Ora Leonard Wildermuth

Wildermuth took a full year of additional work in English, economics, history, and mathematics and was graduated in 1906 with the degree LL.B. During his senior year he was business manager of the *Arbutus* and a member of the debating team. He was admitted to the bar, and at once entered on the practice of law in the rapidly growing city of Gary. He was the city's first teacher, librarian, and attorney.

In 1906 Ora married Cordelia Wilds, of Peru, Indiana. They moved to Gary in 1907 and had one daughter, Maxine (Mrs. Tula). In April, 1941, Mrs. Wildermuth died, and in 1942 Ora married Mae R. London. They were married for ten years when Mae died on March 22, 1952. In June 1955 he married an old family friend Mildred Z. Polak, a graduate of DePauw University (M.S. from IU, 1940), who taught school for many years in the Gary School System. Mildred's sister had been Ora's secretary in 1923.

Wildermuth took an active part in promotion of certain developments taking place among the sand dunes bordering Lake Michigan, where a great industrial center and a modern city were rising, as if by magic. He was a promoter of the Gary Public Library and had been one of its Trustees since its organization in 1908, and the President of the Board since 1913. In 1908 he became the first President of the Gary Bar Association, and from 1916 to 1925 was Chairman of the Committee on Admission to the bar. In 1910 Ora L. Wildermuth became the first City Judge of Gary, an office he held until 1914.

Judge Wildermuth took part in the industrial and business life of Gary. He was Vice-President and Director of Barnes Ice and Coal Company. In 1917–1918 he was a member of the Lake County Council of Defense. In 1933–1934 he was Chairman of the Governor's Committee for Unemployment Relief.

The Judge long had been a member of the American Bar Association, the Indiana State Bar Association, and Lake County Bar Association (President, 1934). He was a member of the American Library Association, which in 1943 awarded him the Citation of Merit of the Association for outstanding service as a library trustee. He had been a Director of the Indiana State Y.M.C.A. since March, 1938.

In 1939 he was President of the Association of Governing Boards of State Universities, secretary since 1943. In June 1936 Wildermuth was one of the founding members and a member of the Board of Directors of the Indiana University Foundation (1936-52; Vice-President, 1936-52; and President, 1938-50), and a Trustee of the Waterman Institute for Scientific Research, Indiana University.

Wildermuth served as a Trustee for twenty-seven years during which time he was Vice-President (1936-38) and President (1938-50) of the Board. Ora was very involved in the planning of the construction that took place on the campus during his era, including building of the fieldhouse that was named for him. A library at Gary also bears his name in honor of his leadership in library development in Gary and throughout the United States. He was one of the founders of the Midwest Interloan Research Library.

In the latter part of his life Wildermuth divided his time between Naples, Florida, and Gary. It was in the latter city that he died November 16, 1964, in Mercy Hospital and was buried in Oak Hills Cemetery, Gary, Indiana. Mildred Wildermuth has continued to reside in Naples since Judge Wildermuth's death.

James Willard Wolfe, 1955–
Student Trustee, 1977–1979

James Willard Wolfe, law student, son of Dudley Anderson and Barbara Blakeman (Lampe) Wolfe, was born in Decatur, Illinois, on August 7, 1955, but became a legal resident of Indiana in 1973. He obtained his B.S. (1977) as an Honors Graduate in the School of Business, the MBA (1979), and J.D. (1981). Jim followed in his older brother Bill's footsteps by attending Indiana University. Bill was on the 1968 Rosebowl football team and went on from Indiana University to become a Rhodes Scholar.

Jim worked as business manager of the *Arbutus* yearbook and was a teaching assistant in the Honors Division. He was a member of the Campus Honors Committee (1974-75), the Indiana University Student Foundation (1975-76), the In-

James Willard Wolfe

diana University Board of Aeons (President in the school year 1976–1977), Sigma Phi Epsilon social fraternity, and was an *Indiana Journal* writer. He is a Presbyterian and was on the 1971 Commission to the General Assembly of the United Presbyterian Church in the USA.

During his college years Jim acquired a number of awards and honors. Among them were his election to Beta Gamma Sigma, business professional honorary; Phi Eta Sigma, men's freshman honorary; Dean's List; Honors Undergraduate Research Grant; and the David Beggs Memorial Scholarship.

During school summer vacations he served as an intern for the Abbott Laboratories in North Chicago, Illinois (1976); worked for the Federal Energy Administration in Washington, DC (1977); the Henry County News, Inc., New Castle, Indiana (1978); and was a law clerk for Bingham, Summers, Welsh, and Spillman in Indianapolis (1979 and 1980). He worked part-time as a consultant to several limited partnerships and small corporations under the auspices of the First Indiana Securities Corporation (1979–81) and as a Research Assistant in the Office of the President at IU (1980–81). He is currently (1982) working in Washington, DC, as a Legislative Director for Senator Dan Quayle.

In 1977 Jim became the second Student Trustee appointed by Governor Bowen for a two-year term.

In addition to his campus activities Jim was interested in photography, camping and traveling.

Presidents

Herman B Wells

Herman B Wells, 1902–

PRESIDENT, 1937–1962

Interim President, September 1, 1968–November 30, 1968

University Chancellor, 1962–

Herman B Wells, educator, was born in Jamestown, Boone County, Indiana, June 7, 1902, son of Joseph Granville and Anna Bernice (Harting) Wells. He completed preparation for college in the Lebanon High School and entered the University of Illinois in the fall of 1920. On completion of the work of the freshman year, he transferred to Indiana University, where he received the B.S. degree in 1924, and in June, 1927, the A.M. degree.

He was assistant cashier, First National Bank, Lebanon (1924–1926); a graduate student at IU (1926–1927); an Assistant in Economics and a graduate student at the University of Wisconsin (1927–1928); a Field Secretary to the Indiana Bankers Association (1928–1931); an Instructor in Economics at Indiana University (1930–1933); and also was Secretary and Research Director of the Study Commission for Indiana Financial Institutions (1931–1933). He was Assistant Professor of Economics, Indiana University (1933–1935), on leave of absence as Supervisor of the Divison of Banks and Trust Companies and Division of Research and Statistics, Department of Financial Institutions of the State of Indiana.

On May 18, 1935, Herman B Wells was appointed Dean of the School of Business Administration, succeeding Dean W. A. Rawles, who had resigned. During the years 1935 to 1972 he also was a Professor of Business Administration.

When William Lowe Bryan resigned as President of Indiana University (June 1937), Herman B Wells was appointed Acting President, effective as of July 1, and on March 22, 1938, he was made President. He was at that time a few months past thirty-six, one of the youngest university presidents in the United States.

President Wells's rapid advancement had not been made by the orthodox route. At the time of his election as President he was more widely known in financial and state government than in academic circles. His extracurricular activities soon became national in scope, however. He was a member of the Board of Directors of the Federal Home Loan Bank of Indianapolis (1936–71, Chairman 1940–71). He was Deputy Director in Charge of Liberated Areas (August 8 to November 6, 1943); Special Advisor on Liberated Areas, U.S. Department of State (November 1943 to February 1944); Consultant to the U.S. Delegation at the San Francisco Conference for the formation of the United Nations (1945); a member of the Allied Mission for Observation of Greek Elections, with rank of Minister (1946); and Advisor on Cultural Affairs to the military governor of Germany, (November 1947–May 1948).

He has served the following organizations: State University Association (President, 1941–42; 1952–53); a member of the Executive Committee of the American Council on Education (Chairman, 1944–1945). He has been a member of the first Board of Regents of American Savings and Loan Institute (Chicago, 1941) and of the Carnegie Foundation for Advancement of Teaching. He holds membership in the Hoosier Art Salon Patrons Association, the National Committee on Public Debt Policy, Brookings Institution, the National Education Association (President of the Division on Higher Education 1943–44), the American Bankers Association (advisory member of Research Council), the Econometric Society, the Indiana Academy of Social Sciences (President, 1934–35), the Indiana Society of Chicago, and the Indiana Society of Pioneers.

His connection with the James Whitcomb Riley Memorial Association began in June, 1938, and he has been Vice-President since January 23, 1941. He was a member of the Board of Directors from January to December, 1941, and has been a member of the Board of Governors (which succeeded the Board of Directors) since December, 1941.

He was Chairman of the Indiana War History Commission and was selected by Durward Howes as one of the nation's "ten outstanding young men of 1939."

Wells has received twenty-seven honorary degrees from various universities and colleges. Among the other honors he has received are Benjamin Franklin Fellow, Royal Society of Arts (London); Fellow, American Academy of Arts and Sciences;

Member, American Philosophical Society, Phi Beta Kappa and Beta Gamma Sigma; The Robins Award of America; Honorary Member, DeMolay Legion of Honor; and Distinguished Alumni Service Award, Indiana University Alumni Association.

He was the author (with others) of the Report of the Study Commission for Indiana Financial Institutions, 1932, and has contributed articles to various publications.

He is a member of numerous social organizations and clubs, among them The University Clubs of New York and Chicago; Cosmos Club (Washington, DC); Century Association (NY); Indiana Academy of Social Sciences (Past President); Mortar Board; Blue Key; Phi Beta Kappa; Kappa Kappa Psi; Sigma Nu social fraternity (regent, 1968–70); Atheneum; Columbia Club; Indianapolis Athletic Club; thirty-third-degree Mason; Kiwanian (honorary); Rotarian (honorary); and Indiana Historical Society (Director, 1968–   ).

When Dr. Wells stepped down as President, he became University Chancellor and continues in that most important and helpful role (1982). He also served as interim President when Elvis Stahr resigned (September 1968), until Joseph Sutton became President (December 1, 1968).

A more complete chronology of Dr. Wells's activities and honors can be found in the Appendix of his biography, *Being Lucky,* published by Indiana University Press in 1980.

Major Events during President Wells's Tenure

1949 Bloomington — Men's Quadrangle (renamed in 1959 Joseph A. Wright Quadrangle) and University Apartments completed. Geological Field Station established in Cardwell, Montana, on sixty acres given by the State of Montana.

1950 Indianapolis — Wing to house research facilities in children's diseases added to Riley Hospital. Laboratory Science Building (renamed in 1959 James W. Fesler Hall) turned over to the Indiana University Medical Center by the State Board of Health.

1951 Bloomington — Wing to University School for School of Education completed. School of Letters established in Graduate School.

1952 Bloomington — New Stores and Service Buildings completed.

1953 Bloomington — Wylie House purchased (restored 1964–65).

Indianapolis — Student Union and Food Service Building at medical Center, Indianapolis, completed.

1954 Bloomington — Wing to Ernie Pyle Hall completed.

Indianapolis — Wing to Riley Hospital for cancer research, and Service and Central Stores Building, Medical Center at Indianapolis, completed.

1955 Bloomington — Jordan Hall of Biology and Smithwood Hall, a dormitory for women, completed. (Smithwood Hall formally

		named Daniel Read Hall in 1961.) Married II complex renamed later to Hepburn, Nutt, Bicknell, Banta Apartments) completed. Material Stores and Salvage Building constructed.
1956	Bloomington	School of Law Building, Beck Chapel, and additional wing to Library completed.
	Southeast	Building for the Southeast Campus at Jeffersonville rebuilt.
1957	Bloomington	Evermann Apartments completed.
1958	Bloomington	Construction of new Stadium, and additions to Swain Hall, School of Music Building, and Field House begun.
	Indianapolis	At Medical Center, Aldred S. Warthin Apartments and Medical Science Building completed.
	Fort Wayne	IU-PU Foundation established.
1959	Bloomington	Construction of Fine Arts and Radio and Television Building begun. Lilly Library, Ballantine Hall, Tower Quadrangle (renamed in 1961 Nellie S. Teter Quadrangle), and Biddle Continuation Center addition to Indiana Memorial Union completed. Construction begun on two additional apartment buildings in the Evermann apartments area. Land and buildings of the former Showers Brothers Company purchased for University use.
	Indianapolis	At Medical Center addition to Dentistry begun. Division of Allied Health Sciences established in School of Medicine.
	Northwest	New building for Gary Center completed.

	South Bend	New building for South Bend-Mishawaka Center begun.
1960	Bloomington	Construction on Lilly Library, Football Stadium, Athletic Field House, Swain Hall addition, School of Music addition, and Married Students Apartments IV (renamed in 1961 Redbud Hill Apartments) completed. Addition made to Kirkwood Observatory.
1961	Bloomington	Graduate School of Business established. Construction completed on the School of Health, Physical Education and Recreation Building, also Woodlawn Dormitories and Ruby E. C. Mason Hall; the Showalter Fountain dedicated. Crooked Lake Biological Station, twenty-seven acres, acquired.
	Indianapolis	Dental School addition in Indianapolis completed.
	South Bend	South Bend Campus moved to present site; Northside Hall opened.

Elvis Jacob Stahr, Jr., 1916–
PRESIDENT, 1962–1968

Elvis Jacob Stahr, Jr., lawyer and educator, son of Elvis Jacob and Mary Anne (McDaniel) Stahr, was born in Hickman, Kentucky, on March 9, 1916. He attended school in Hickman through high school, where he was valedictorian of his 1932 graduating class. He received his A.B. (1936) from the University of Kentucky "with High Distinction" and was elected to Phi Beta Kappa. He was co-captain of both the tennis and debate teams at Kentucky, as well as president of his class and his fraternity. He also was a cadet colonel of the ROTC. A Rhodes Scholar, he obtained a B.A. in Jurisprudence (1938), Bachelor of Civil Law (1939), and an M.A. (1943) from Oxford University in England.

He entered the practice of law in New York (July 1939) but was called to active duty in the Army. He attended the Infantry School at Fort Benning, Georgia (October 1941–1942), then obtained a diploma in Chinese Language from Yale University (1943) and spent more than two years overseas, principally in China, emerging as a Lieutenant Colonel. He was awarded four US medals, including the bronze star with oak leaf cluster, several battle stars and service ribbons, as well as three medals from the Chinese Army.

After the war he returned to New York and practiced law until he joined the University of Kentucky law faculty (June 1947).

Before leaving New York, however, Elvis married Dorothy Howland Berkfield of New York City on June 28, 1946, and they had three children; Stephanie Ann (graduated from Smith and University of Virginia Law School), Stuart Edward Winston, and Bradford Lanier Stahr (the two boys attended Indiana University).

At Kentucky, Stahr rose from Associate Professor of Law to full Professor in 1948 and later that year was named Dean of the College of Law. In 1954 he took on the additional duties of Provost of the University. During his Kentucky tenure, he took three leaves of absence for three months each to serve as a Special Assistant to the Secretary of the Army and to be a

Elvis Jacob Stahr, Jr.

consultant to the Assistant Secretary of the Army for manpower. During the academic year 1956–1957 he served as the Executive Director of President Eisenhower's Committee on Education beyond the High School.

In July 1957 he became Vice-Chancellor for the Professional Schools and Professor of Law at the University of Pittsburgh and then moved on to the presidency of West Virginia University in August 1958.

Elvis started to pick up honors early, receiving the George Washington Bicentennial Medal for first place in a state essay contest in 1932. He was given the Algernon Sydney Sullivan Medallion by the University of Kentucky and the Balfour National Award of Sigma Chi Fraternity in 1936. He was elected to the Order of the Coif, Sigma Chi (in which he held several offices between 1935 and 1955), Omicron Delta Kappa, Tau Kappa Alpha, Merton Society (Oxford), and honorary memberships in Phi Delta Phi, Alpha Kappa Psi, Blue Key, and Beta Gamma Sigma. In 1948 he was voted "One of the Ten Outstanding Young Men of America." He became a Kentucky Colonel (1935), and a Kentucky General (1961), a Louisiana Admiral (1961), and a Nebraska Admiral (1962). The year 1961 was crowded with honors: Stahr received the Sigma Chi "Significant Sig" award, The Order of Grand Cruz (Peru), and the Kentucky Press Association's "Kentuckian of the Year" award. In 1962 the ROTC gave him their Distinguished Service Award, and the Comanche Indian Tribe in Oklahoma made him an honorary member. He is an honorary member of the Strawberry Hill Cannoneers and the Indiana State Bar Association and has received twenty-seven honorary doctorates.

Stahr has held membership in numerous organizations, among them the Sons of the American Revolution, Newcomen Society, American Legion, American and Kentucky Bar Associations, American Law Institute, Institute of Judicial Administration. He has served on numerous government committees at the state and federal level. He was a charter member of the Federal Bar Association Foundation and of the University of Kentucky Library Associates, as well as the first President of the latter. He was Director of the Southern Regional Education Board (1959-61), West Virginia Chamber of Commerce (1959-1961), Morgantown, West Virginia Chamber of Commerce (1959-1961), and Panama Canal Company (1961-1962). He served as trustee of the Claude Worthington Benedum Foundation (1959-1961) and the American University Field Staff (1962-1968), and was a member of the Ford Motor Company Scholarship Board Association of the United States Army (three terms as President) and Chairman of the Board of the Indiana University Foundation (1962-1968).

Stahr has served on the boards of the Chase Manhatten Bank, Federal Reserve Bank of Chicago (Deputy Chairman), Acacia Mutual Life Insurance Company (member, Executive Committee), First National Bank of Morgantown, West Virginia, Saxon Industries, Inc., and General Computing Corporation.

In addition to his many military and educational involvements, Elvis found time over the years for many civic activities. He is a Life Senator of the Junior Chamber International; was Chairman of the Red Cross Fund Drive in Lexington, Kentucky, in 1951. An Honorary Member of the National Council of the Boy Scouts of America, Stahr was involved in several other civic committees in Kentucky and Pennsylvania during the 1950s. He served on the boards of the American Cancer Society, National Association of Educational Broadcasters, and the Committee for Economic Development. While at Indiana, Elvis also was a member of the Board of Governors of the James Whitcomb Riley Memorial Association (1962-68).

As President of Indiana University, Stahr also served as Chairman of the Board of the IU Foundation (1962-68), a member of the Council of Ten (1962-68),* Trustee of American Universities Field Staff (1962-68; Vice-Chairman, 1964; Chairman, 1966-68), a member of the Executive Committee of the Indiana Conference on Higher Education (1963-66; President, 1964-65) and co-chairman, with President Hovde of Purdue, of Governor Branigan's Committee for Nuclear Accelerator Site (1965). He served on various committees of

---

*The Council of Ten is a quasi-consortium of the presidents of all the Big Ten Universities—Illinois, Indiana, Iowa, Ohio, Michigan, Michigan State, Minnesota, Northwestern, Purdue, Wisconsin—plus the University of Chicago.

the State Universities Association and Association of American Universities (1962–68), was a trustee for Tudor Hall School (1963–69), the Midwestern Universities Research Association President (1963–65) and a member of National Association of State Universities and Land Grant Colleges (Equal Opportunity Committee 1965–68).

Due to his numerous home-base locations Stahr has had a wide variety of social-club memberships, including the Cosmos Club and Army-Navy Club in Washington, DC, the Columbia Club, Indianapolis Athletic Club, Woodstock Club, University Club and Athenaeum Club. He also has belonged to the Rotary in Lexington, Kentucky and in Morgantown, West Virginia; the Oxford Carlton Club in England; the West Side Tennis Club, Forest Hills, Long Island; the University Club in Pittsburgh; and has honorary membership in both the Indiana Society of Chicago and the Filson Club of Louisville (an honor society of Kentucky Mountain Men).

Elvis was reared as a member of the Disciples of Christ Church and was formerly a deacon in the Central Christian Church in Lexington, Kentucky, and an elder in the First Christian Churches in Morgantown, West Virginia, and Bloomington, Indiana.

Stahr was appointed Secretary of the Army (January 1961) and held that position until he became President of Indiana University (July 1, 1962).

He resigned as President of Indiana University on August 31, 1968, and became President of the National Audubon Society, serving until 1979, when he became Senior Counselor. He was elected President Emeritus (1981) and that same year became President of University Associates, Inc.

Major Events during President Stahr's Tenure

1962 Bloomington Elvis Stahr named President of Indiana University. Fine Arts Building, Geology Building, Campus View House (married student housing), Residence Halls Administration completed. Additional land and buildings of the former Showers Brothers Company, furniture manufacturers, at Tenth and Morton acquired for warehouse space and other purposes.

     South Bend The South Bend-Mishawaka Campus Building completed.

1963 Bloomington Psychology Building, Administrative Services Building, Graduate Student Dormitory, Radio and Television Building and the John W. Foster Quadrangle completed. The "Ole Swimmin' Hole" dedicated at Bradford Woods. Crosstown Shopping Center purchased by University Foundation.

     Northwest Gary and Calumet campuses combined under a single administration with facilities to be known as Northwest Campus.

1964 Bloomington Construction completed on Paul V. McNutt Quadrangle, University Schools complex, Chemistry Building addition, Geological Survey (an addition to the Geology Building). Construction on the following facilities was started: Fee Lane

		West II (now Briscoe Quadrangle for single students), Health Center, Business and Economics building, outdoor swimming pools, Forest Quadrangle. Nurre factory purchased. Addition made to Myers Hall. Remodeling done on old University Schools area in Education Building. Cedar Hall demolished; Pine and Laurel Halls converted to academic use.
	Fort Wayne	A new building (Kettler Hall) at Fort Wayne completed (building to be used jointly with Purdue University).
1965	Bloomington	Division of General and Technical Studies established. Construction completed on Wendell L. Willkie Quadrangle, Boiler Plant addition, outdoor swimming pool and Married VI (named Tulip Tree House).
	Indianapolis	Ground broken for new teaching hospital at Medical Center.
	Kokomo	Kokomo Campus Building completed.
	Southeast	Old post office in Jeffersonville purchased as addition to Southeast Campus.
1966	Bloomington	School of Religion Building on Union Street purchased (now houses News Bureau). Construction begun on new Library at Tenth and Jordan; Optometry Building, Atwater Avenue; and Eigenmann Center, Tenth and Union. Construction completed on Student Health Center at Tenth and Jordan (old Health Center, Howe House, used temporarily for academic offices), Forest Quadrangle, and Briscoe Quadrangle. Twenty acres, eight miles east on East

		Third Street, purchased for research activity of Department of Zoology. The regional campuses separated, in March, from the Division of University Extension and organized under the Division of Regional Campus Administration. Construction completed on the Observatory, Morgan Monroe State Forest, and on the new School of Business Building. Remodeling completed on Material Stores; Salvage Building on Eleventh Street converted to controlled temperature building for Audio-Visual tape storage. Fourth floor of Swain Hall West enlarged by ten rooms. Shelter House built for Beechwood Heights. Part of main floor of Goodbody Hall remodeled to accommodate History and Philosophy of Science; remodeling in progress at Morrison Hall for Biological Sciences. Arbutus and Maple Halls taken over from Halls of Residence for academic use. Twenty-one of Hoosier Courts complex scheduled for demolition.
	Indianapolis	Ransburg Building, 630 West New York Street, remodeled for central stores.
	South Bend	Greenwood Hall opened.
1967	Bloomington	Showers Factory #2 and Nurre Factory demolished. Two hundred forty-five acres on Monroe Reservoir acquired to house Biological Research Station. Construction started on Speech and Hearing Clinic. Optometry Building scheduled for completion in fall. Remodeling completed on Morrison Hall.
	Indianapolis	Berkey's market in Indianapolis re-

	modeled for Medical Center Data Processing Area. Riley remodeling (Hospital Surgery addition and Biochemistry) almost completed.
Northwest	Planning at Gary started on Auditorium Building, classroom building, and addition to existing structure.
South Bend	I.U. conferred first degrees at a South Bend commencement.

Joseph Lee Sutton

Joseph Lee Sutton, 1924-1972
PRESIDENT, 1968-1971
Vice-President and
Dean of Faculties
1966-1968

Joseph Lee Sutton, educator and Far-East specialist, son of Erville C. and Carolyn E. (Hatch) Sutton (later Mrs. Gilbert Simmonds), was born March 22, 1924, in Oklahoma City, Oklahoma. He came from a journalistic family and originally thought his field of endeavor would be in the same area. His grandfather and his great uncle, Elmer and Wilber Sutton, had founded *The Muncie Press*. Later his grandfather moved to Indiana territory and founded a newspaper in what was to become Bartlesville, Oklahoma. His father was editor of the latter paper.

Joe went to school in Oklahoma including the first year of college at Oklahoma State University. He entered the Army in 1943, and his aptitude for languages sent him to the University of Michigan, under the auspices of military intelligence, where he studied Japanese. He was commissioned a Lieutenant and served as a Japanese language officer in General MacArthur's headquarters in Tokyo. Shortly before leaving for Japan, Joe married Jean Harkness of Grand Rapids, Michigan, on August 19, 1945, and they had four children: James, Jeffrey, David, and Abigail.

After discharge from the Army, Sutton returned to the University of Michigan and obtained his A.B. in Oriental Languages (1948), an A.M. in Oriental Civilization (1949), and a Ph.D. in Political Science (1954). Meanwhile he was a Social Science Research Council Fellow in 1951-1952 and spent the time in Japan gathering material on Japanese politics. While working on his Ph.D. dissertation, Joe became a Lecturer at Western Reserve University in Cleveland, Ohio, during the school year 1952-1953, and then in 1953 joined the faculty of Indiana University. He rose steadily through the academic ranks and became a full Professor in 1962. Joe was an outstanding teacher and early in his career had been awarded the

Sigma Delta Chi's "Brown Derby" as the most popular professor (1955). In 1955, Sutton went to Thailand as Chief of Party to set up a School of Public Administration at Thammasart University in Bangkok. After his return to Bloomington he became involved in a series of administrative positions, in addition to his teaching tasks. He moved from Chairman of the Asian Studies Program to Associate Dean, then to Dean of the College of Arts and Sciences, and eventually to Vice-President and Dean of Faculties (1966 to 1968). On December 1, 1968, he became President, taking over from Acting-President and Chancellor Herman B Wells.

Sutton was an outstanding public speaker and often was called upon to speak to various organizations in both the academic and public communities. He had served as a consultant to the Ford Foundation and Carnegie Corporation, and was a member of the three-man National Committee to plan an observance of the "International Year of the Arts and Humanities in 1970," which was suggested by President Lyndon Johnson.

Joe was a member of the American Political Science Association, Far Eastern Association, American Council of Learned Societies, Riley Memorial Association, Council of Ten, Association of American Universities, the Columbia Club, Indianapolis Athletic Club, White Lake Golf Club and the White Lake Yacht Club, the latter two in Whitehall, Michigan.

After the death of wife, Jean, he resigned the presidency in order to spend more time with his children. He married Elizabeth Josephson of Moline, Illinois, in March 1971. They were due to leave for Japan, where Joe was to be the first exchange Professor at Tenri University on an interinstitutional program for Indiana University, when they were involved in an automobile accident which resulted in Joe's death. He was buried in Oklahoma City, Oklahoma, on May 1, 1972.

Major Events during President Sutton's Tenure

1968 Bloomington — Herman B Wells, Interim President. Joseph Lee Sutton named President of the University. Construction completed on the new Optometry Building on Atwater Avenue and on Speech and Hearing Clinic. Construction in progress on the new Library area, Eigenmann Center at Tenth and Union, Musical Arts Center, Mentally Retarded Research Center in the University Schools complex, Food Storage Building in the Showers complex, Morgan, Linden, and Hickory Halls. One wing of Memorial Hall converted to academic use. Plans underway for a Chilled Water Plant, Learning and Resources Center, and Accelerator Building. East Hall and small ballet building razed by fire.

Indianapolis — Construction completed on the Preventive Dentistry Research Building and University Hospital Phase I; construction begun on Riley Hospital Mentally Retarded Section; bids requested for the new Regional Campus Center, consisting of three buildings, and also for the new Law Building and University Hospital, Phase II. Herron School of Art affiliated with IU.

Northwest — Construction completed on two temporary transitional buildings and work begun on two additions to the main campus building (library and faculty

	areas) and on a student services and an academic building.
South Bend	Construction completed on the addition of student lounge and bookstore areas to the main building.
Southeast	One temporary office structure completed at Southeast (Jeffersonville).
1969 Bloomington	John W. Ryan named Vice-President for Regional Campuses. Construction in Bloomington completed on New Library, Eigenmann Graduate Residence Center, Food Storage, Retarded Center Addition to University School, Chilled Water Plant. Student uprisings; two fires cause extensive damage to old Library. Sigma Alpha Epsilon and Delta Chi fraternity houses demolished.
Indianapolis	Building at 1217 West Michigan bought for offices of the Chancellor of Indiana University at Indianapolis. IU and PU merged into IUPUI, with IU given administrative and fiscal control.
Northwest	Additions made which included campus student activities, academic and library facilities.
South Bend	Greenlawn Hall completed with faculty offices and classrooms for Dental Hygiene.
1970 Bloomington	Construction underway for Assembly Hall, accelerator building (north of Bypass), Office of Publications Building at Rogers and Eleventh Streets, the Glenn Black Laboratory at Ninth and Fess, and the Musical Arts building. The new Credit Union building at Seventeenth and Dunn Streets completed.

	The University School complex leased to the Monroe County Community School System. A Museum at Angel Mounds archeological site, under construction.
Indianapolis	Herron School of Art, owned by the Art Association, joined with IU as of September, 1970 (thirty-five studios, four galleries, and library). Completion expected on three regional buildings. A fourth regional building underway. Bids taken in the fall for Phase II of University Hospital. A Medicine Research Facility Building under construction; also an addition to the School of Dentistry facilities. School of Law, Indianapolis, dedicated.
South Bend	Work begun on the auditorium addition to the main building with completion expected in two years.
Southeast	Plans formulated for a new regional campus at New Albany.
Columbus	Center officially opened.

John William Ryan

John William Ryan 1929–
PRESIDENT, 1971–
Vice President and Chancellor for Regional Campuses, 1969–1970
Vice-President and Dean for Regional
Campuses, 1968–1969

John William Ryan, political scientist, educator, and administrator, son of Leonard John and Maxine Mary (Mitchell) Ryan, was born in Chicago on August 12, 1929, and attended grammar school there. His family moved to Minnesota, and John graduated from Loyola High School in Mankato (1947). He then took his B.A. at the University of Utah (1951).

While in Salt Lake, John met and married D. Patricia Goodday on March 21, 1948. They have three children: Kathleen Elynne (Mrs. Kevin Acker, B.S. 1974; Mr. Acker B.S. 1972, MBA 1973); Kevin Dennis Mitchell (B.S., Purdue, 1978); Kerrick Charles Casey (B.S., Arizona State University, 1979; M.A., IU 1982).

Upon completion of his degree at Utah, John and his family moved to Bloomington where he began work on the Ph.D. and was a graduate assistant in the Government Department (1952–54). He interrupted his graduate study and moved to Frankfurt, Kentucky, to work as a research analyst in the Kentucky Department of Revenue (1954–55). Indiana University invited him to serve as Visiting Research Professor, joining the group which went to Bangkok, Thailand, to establish the Institute of Public Administration in collaboration with Thammasart University (1955–1957). Upon his return to Bloomington to finish his Ph.D. dissertation, Ryan became Assistant Director of the Institute for Training for Public Service (1957–58). His M.A. was awarded in 1958 and his Ph.D. in 1959. Meanwhile Ryan had accepted an appointment as Assistant Professor of Political Science at the University of Wisconsin (1958–60) and was promoted to Associate Professor in 1960. This was the first of his moves out of Bloomington that would have him crisscrossing the country to accept increasingly more responsible positions. He left the University of Wisconsin (1962) to become Assistant to the President and Secretary of the University of Massachusetts at Amherst for two years. In 1963, Arizona State University at Tempe offered John the position of Vice-President for Academic Affairs and Professor of Political Science with tenure. He remained at Arizona until 1965, when the Trustees of the University of Massachusetts asked him to return to set up a new campus in Boston, where he assumed the position of Chancellor.

Ryan's alma mater called for his return in 1968 to become Vice-President for Regional Campuses and Professor of Government, with tenure. The title of his position changed, as reorganization of the University progressed, from Vice-President and Dean for Regional Campuses (October 1968) to Vice-President and Chancellor for Regional Campuses (July 1969). In January 1971 President Joseph Sutton terminated his own short tenure in office with a sudden resignation. The Trustees determined that an immediate appointment to the unexpectedly vacant presidency was required in the vital interest of the University. After a flurry of meetings and consultations with many members of the faculty, the alumni, and the leadership of the state, the Trustees decided, at a special Board of Trustees meeting, to elect Ryan to the position. He accepted the office for a three-year term. He became President on January 26, 1971, although his formal investiture did not take place until January 20, 1972. When Ryan was appointed President, he stipulated with the Trustees that his appointment be for three years and then be evaluated. At his behest, such evaluations have taken place twice (1973 and 1978).

While at Utah, John became a Kappa Sigma and later was named their "Man of the Year" (1975); a more recent national honor was bestowed by his fraternity when he was elected Worthy Grand Master of Ceremonies (1981). Other honors that have been bestowed upon him include honorary degrees from The College of St. Thomas (D. Litt. 1977), University of Notre Dame (LL.D. 1977), Oakland City College (LL.D. 1981), St. Joseph College (LL.D. 1981), and Hanover College (LL.D. 1982). The Boys Club Association of Indianapolis honored Ryan with the Horatio Alger Award (1980); he received the Sagamore of the Wabash from Governor Otis R. Bowen (1975) and has been elected to the Indiana Academy (1980) and to the honoraries of Beta Gamma Sigma and Pi Alpha Alpha. Ryan also has received the highest honor awarded a Catholic, layman or clergy, when he was named a Knight of the Equestrian Order of the Holy Sepulchre of Jerusalem. Although this honor was designated in 1981, he was unable to attend the ceremony because of an Indiana University commencement commitment, and his investiture was deferred to May 1, 1982.

Prior to his appointment as President, Ryan published numerous articles and monographs on public administration and local government in Thailand, as well as on various aspects of public administration in the United States, and a number of politically-oriented articles relating to public administration.

As President, Ryan has held memberships and innumerable offices in organizations associated with academia such as the Air University Board of Visitors (AFIT) (1974–81; Chairman, AFIT Subcommittee, 1976–81); American Council on Education (1971–); American Judicature Society (1975–); American Political Science Association (1952–); American Society for Public Administration (1952–; President, Indiana Chapter, 1969–70; National Council Member, 1970–; National President, 1972–73); American Universities Field Staff (1971–; Chairman of the Board, 1972–77); Association of American Universities (member of Health Education Committee, 1978–81; Executive Committee 1971–, Chairman, 1981–82); Association for Asian Studies (1958–); College of St. Thomas (Trustee 1975–; Chairman, Committee on Academic and Student Affairs, 1980–; Chairman, MBA Review Committee, 1980–); Council for Financial Aid to Education (Director, 1981–); Council of Ten (Committee on Institutional Cooperation; Representative to NCAA, 1980–; Chairman, 1981–); Indiana Center for Advanced Research (1974–; Director, 1977–80); Indiana Conference of Higher Education (President, 1977–78; Executive Committee, 1977–); Indiana Newman Foundation (Director, 1969; President, 1969–71); Indiana Revolutionary Bicentennial Commission (1976–81); Indiana University Foundation (Chairman of the Board, 1972–); American Council of Life Insurance (formerly Life Insurance

Institute; member, University Advisory Council (1977–; Chairman, 1982); Inter-University Centre at Dubrovnik, Yugoslavia (Executive Committee, 1981–); Midwest Universities Consortium for International Activities (Council of Presidents, 1971–; Chairman 1976–78, 1981–); National Academy of Public Administration, National Association of State Universities and Land-Grant Colleges (Committee on Education for Business Professions, 1976–78; Veterans Affairs Committee, 1977–) Council of Presidents, Joint Committee on Health Policy (with AAU and ACE 1978–81; Division of Urban Affairs, 1980–; Chairman, International Affairs Committee, 1980–); National Institute for Campus Ministries (Director, 1975–78; member, Development Committee); North Central Association of Colleges and Secondary Schools (Executive Board of Committee on Higher Education, 1976–81); PBS (Board of Governors, 1973–82; Chairman, PTV-3 Committee, 1980–82; Executive Committee, 1980–82); CPB (member of the Annenberg Committee, 1981–82); Riley Memorial Association (Board of Governors, 1971–).

Ryan's contributions, which also have some University implications, have included service on the Mayor's Bloomington Community Progress Council (1980–); Corporate Community Council, Indianapolis (director, 1976–); and the Governor's White River Park Commission (1979–).

Ryan also serves as a Director of the Indiana Bell Telephone Company (1972–; Chairman of its Corporate Public Policy Advisory Committee, 1979–; member of the Auditing Committee, 1979–) and of the State Life Insurance Company. He holds memberships in the Indiana Societies of Chicago (nonresident Vice-President, 1976–), New York, and Washington; Bloomington Rotary, Elks, Quail Ridge Golf and Tennis Club, Indianapolis Athletic Club, Columbia Club, Meridian Hills Country Club, Skyline Club, Cosmos Club (Washington, DC), Explorer's Club (New York), Newcomen Society, Knights of Columbus, the University Clubs at Indiana University, Boston, and New York City, the honorary fraternities of Pi Sigma Alpha, Phi Kappa Phi, and Phi Alpha Theta.

Major Events during President Ryan's Tenure

1971	Bloomington	Ryan named President, following resignation of Joseph L. Sutton. Buildings completed: Assembly Hall (Arena), Metz Carillon, Musical Arts Center, Glenn Black Laboratory, Publications, Accelerator Building, and the new high-rise parking garage on Atwater. Major remodeling: Chemistry Phase IV; Curry Bookstore (leased) remodeled for use as an annex by the Registrar; one half of Coulter Hall converted to Exchange House; Sycamore; and the old Library.
	Indianapolis	IUPUI Regional Buildings accepted; Medical Research Facilities Building and Riley Addition, Phase II completed. Medical Science Building remodeled. Under construction or planning: Dental School Addition; School of Nursing; University Hospital Phase IIA; Science Engineering and Technology; Administration and Krannert (a classroom, laboratory, and office building). Normal College of the American Gymnastic Union moved to 1010 West 46th (later named School of Physical Education).
	Kokomo	Major remodeling of basement area to provide office space.
	Southeast	Southeast Campus at New Albany started.
1972	Bloomington	Poplars Hotel at Dunn and Seventh Streets purchased (now Poplars Re-

		search and Conference Center). Old Library Building renovated as Student Services Building. SPEA established.
	Indianapolis	Dental School Addition dedicated.
	Fort Wayne	Neff Hall and Helmke Library completed.
	South Bend	Northside Hall Addition completed.
1973	Bloomington	Razed: Hoosier Courts Apartments and Nursery, Old Audio-Visual (Rogers) Building, Howe House, Old Radio and Television Building. Building at 109 North Jordan remodeled for the new Black Culture Center. The Senior High Building of University School taken over by the Department of Education and renamed Henry Lester Smith Research Center. Road leading to Physics Accelerator Building named the Milo B. Sampson Lane, memorializing the late physics professor.
	Indianapolis	Nursing Building accepted in August.
	Southeast	Southeast Campus at New Albany opened.
	Fort Wayne	Walb Memorial Union completed.
1974	Bloomington	Major administrative reorganization. Regional Administration is phased out, Bloomington and Indianapolis recognized as the core campus. Radio and Television Department changed name to Department of Telecommunications; Department of Journalism changed to School of Journalism within the College of Arts and Sciences. Ernie Pyle Hall out of service to allow extensive remodeling (first floor finished 1975). IU Foundation constructs new building, called

		Showalter House, on Bypass 46 near IU golf course. Razed: Hickory, Maple, and Laurel Halls.
	Indianapolis	Establishment of the IUPUI Vice-President in the former Lilly Mansion. New Administration Service Building accepted. Phase IIA, University Hospital completed; includes the Nuclear Medicine Area, which will house two linear accelerators. Science Engineering and Technology Building still under construction. Long Hospital first floor completely renovated. It now houses doctors and clinics for outpatients. Mannechoir building sold.
	Richmond	Richmond facility occupied.
	Fort Wayne	IU and PU at Fort Wayne unified under one Chancellor.
1975	Bloomington	Optometry Division redesignated as a School. Indiana University Cyclotron Facility on Milo B. Sampson Lane ready for use. Wildermuth Intramural Center being remodeled; an intramural football field north of Fee Lane tennis courts under construction.
	Richmond	New building at IU East now in use.
	Indianapolis	Administration Building completed. Coleman Hospital vacated, moved into new University Hospital Addition. Engineering and Technology Building completed.
	South Bend	Associates' Complex acquired.
	Southeast	Southeast campus at New Albany continues to build. Hillside Hall and the Life Science Building completed.

1976	Bloomington	Multipurpose floor installed in Wildermuth Fieldhouse. Lighted fields prepared for intramural football and baseball at Fee Lane and 46 Bypass. Foundation acquires land on shore of Lake Monroe to be used as a recreational area. Basketball team, under direction of Bobby Knight, wins 1975–76 NCAA championship. Bryan Hall remodeled.
	Indianapolis	Wilson Street parking garage completed. Winona Village taken out of service. Camp Riley dormitory facilities expanded: six cabins, dining hall, boys' and girls' bath house, craft house, as well as staff and infirmary facilities.
	Northwest	Laboratory-classroom building and chilled water facility completed.
	Southeast	Student Activities Building completed.
1977	Bloomington	President's residence, Bryan House, renovated and remodeled; Phase II of the Ernie Pyle Hall renovation completed; renovation of the Indiana Memorial Union Commons completed; new Geology Core Storage Building opened. Andrew Wylie House entered on the National Register of Historic Places. Honeywell House at Wabash reconstructed and dedicated.
	Richmond	New IHETS TV tower installed.
	Indianapolis	Riley Hospital Intensive Care Clinic completed.
	Northwest	305 West 35th Avenue apartment building renovated and remodeled for academic use.

		South Bend	IUSB moved into sections of Associates' Properties.

1978 Bloomington — New Central Energy Management placed in operation; Animal Care Building completed; major renovation of Indiana Memorial Union Cafeteria completed; Fine Arts Museum and Academic Building started. *Breaking Away* filmed.

      Indianapolis — Nuclear Medicine renovation completed; Classroom/Office Building #1 (Business/SPEA) started.

      Northwest — Major remodeling of Tamarack Hall completed.

1979 Bloomington — Music Practice Building completed; new Golf Course Clubhouse dedicated; School of Business addition and remodeling started; major pollution control systems added to Central Power Plant. Old Crescent buildings (including Student Service Building, Student Building, Maxwell Hall, Owen Hall, Wylie Hall, Kirkwood Hall, Lindley Hall, the Rose Well House and Kirkwood Observatory) listed on the Indiana Registrar of Historic Places. School of Education Building officially named the Wendell W. Wright School of Education Building. Indiana won the NIT championship in basketball. Indiana played in the Holiday Bowl in San Diego, winning IU's first bowl victory in football. World Premiere of *Breaking Away* in Bloomington.

      Indianapolis — Tenth Anniversary of IUPUI celebrated. Indianapolis Sports Center completed.

1980	Bloomington	Kirkwood Observatory renovated; total restoration of Woodburn Hall completed; SPEA addition to School of Business and new "Little 500" and Soccer Stadium started; new Visitors Center opened in remodeled former Golf Clubhouse; partial renovation of Chemistry Building and Wylie Hall completed; Hoosier Heritage Phase II, Mathers Museum, started. Old Crescent buildings listed on the National Register of Historic Places. Four residence halls officially named: Graduate Residence Center became the John W. Ashton Center, Building "A" of the Herman T. Briscoe Quadrangle became Frank T. Gucker Hall, Building "B" became Raymond L. Shoemaker Hall, and the Men's Residence Center/Living-Learning Center became the Ralph L. Collins Living-Learning Center.
	Fort Wayne	Ground broken for Athletic Center; faculty approved new constitution for a single faculty senate.
	Indianapolis	Riley Hospital Pediatric Cardiac Catheterization Clinic and Laboratory completed; Engineering and Technology Building Computer Facility finished; renovation of Coleman Hall finished; Parking Garages Michigan East and South opened; two-story vertical addition to Medical Science Building completed; construction of three major intensive care units started. Gymnasium/Natatorium started on the sites of the Beveridge Paper Company and the American Baking Company facilities which were demolished.

		Ground broken for Classroom II. Von Schlegell Sculpture in University Courtyard dedicated.
	Kokomo	New Classroom/Laboratory/Office Building completed and occupied.
	Northwest	New Library/Conference Center dedicated. Contracts let for landscaping and site development.
	Southeast	Activities Building dedicated.
1981	Bloomington	School of Music students presented week-long series of performances in New York City, including first performance by a university company at the Metropolitan Opera House. Little 500/Soccer Stadium opened; new football practice fields placed in service; Fine Arts Museum and Academic Building completed, Library sections of School of Business Addition occupied; Lake Monroe Alumni Family Camp started; extensive landscaping projects completed; University Landscape Nursery placed in service; complete new hardwood playing courts and new running track completed in Wildermuth Intramural Center; major modifications and improvements of University Cyclotron Facility completed. School of Journalism became system-wide school.
	Richmond	Tenth anniversary of Richmond campus celebrated.
	Indianapolis	Classroom/Office I dedicated; construction started on Stadium/Playing Field complex; University Townhouses completed and occupied; major landscaping, entryway and street tree-planting com-

	pleted; RTU, SICU, and CICU intensive care units and associated materials transport system completed in University Hospital; construction of Ronald McDonald House started.
Southeast	Fortieth anniversary of Southeast campus celebrated.
Fort Wayne	Trustees of IU and PU recognized constitution joining IU and PU faculties under one governing body. Medical Education Program established in School of Medicine.
1982 Bloomington	Memorial service held for composer and IU Alumnus Hoagy Carmichael. Composer/conductor Leonard Bernstein in residence on campus as first fellow of Institute for Advanced Study. School of Music staged *The Passion Play* at the Cloisters in New York City. First formal exhibit held in Indiana University Art Museum honoring donors James S. and Elizabeth G. Adams. Indiana University Art Museum dedicated. Additions to Administrative and Academic Computing initiated; revised campus phone system in use. William Hammond Mathers Museum (Hoosier Heritage Center) completed; addition to School of Business Building housing School of Public and Environmental Affairs and joint Business/SPEA library dedicated; Lake Monroe Family Camp completed; Tenth Street Stadium razed, landscaping begun on site; Central Chilled Water service extended to central campus; additions to Jordan Hall begun; addition to Service Building completed; Physical

	Plant Grounds Building completed. Ground broken for Bloomington Law School Addition. Nuclear Theory Center dedicated; American Studies Program in Yugoslavia (IU/Zagreb University) dedicated.
Indianapolis	Business/SPEA Building dedicated; Natatorium/Gymnasium and Track and Field Stadium completed and dedicated; U.S. Sports Festival and other national and international contests held in new facilities; Classroom/Office II (School of Education and School of Social Work) and Ronald McDonald House completed and dedicated; University Hospital lobby and cafeteria remodeled; remodeling of Union Building completed; parking lots rebuilt and landscaped. Inauguration of School of Journalism.
Fort Wayne	Athletic Center and Classroom/Office Building dedicated.
Kokomo	Fifteen acres acquired adjacent to campus. Library area expanded.
Northwest	Medical Education Building, Tamarack Hall, Raintree Hall, and Moraine Student Center renovated.

Vice Presidents

John William Ashton

John William Ashton, 1900–1971
Vice-President, 1952–1965

John William Ashton, educator, author, and Shakespearean scholar, son of Albert William and Hattie Manetta (Flower) Ashton, was born in Lewiston, Maine, on July 11, 1900. His early education took place in Maine, and he took his A.B. degree from Bates College (1922), which later honored him with an LL.D. (1952). He obtained his Ph.D. from the University of Chicago (1928).

Upon receipt of his A.B., he moved to Yankton, South Dakota, where he became an Instructor in English and Speech at Yankton College. He moved on to the University of Iowa in 1923 and remained there until 1940, having attained the rank of Associate Professor of English. A full professorship in 1940 at the University of Kansas led to the chairmanship of the English Department, from which he departed in 1945 to become the head of the English Branch of Shrivenham American University in England.

During his early years at the University of Iowa, Ashton spent some time at the University of Chicago finishing his Ph.D. On November 1, 1925, he married Florence Elizabeth Huber, and they had two daughters: Elizabeth (Mrs. Edward J. Costello, A.B. in English 1949; Mr. Costello, B.S. in Business 1949) and Mary Beatrice (Mrs. Richard Bell, A.B. 1954; Mr. Bell, B.S. in Business 1954). The Bell's son, Richard, is currently (1982) a student at IU.

Ashton made his last university move in February 1946, when he became Dean of the College of Arts and Sciences (and Professor of English) at Indiana University. In 1951 his title and job changed to that of Dean and Director of Student and Educational Services. He held this position until June 1958. Along with his other duties, he became the Vice-President in 1952. As Dean of Arts and Sciences, Ashton was greatly responsible for developing the university's Area Studies program, which combined the offerings of various departments for specialized studies.

During the summer of 1951 John assumed the leadership and guidance of the School of Letters, which was a continuation of the Kenyon School of English held at Kenyon College in the summers of 1948–50, with a grant from the Rockefeller Foundation. When the grant terminated, the Senior Fellows of the Kenyon School of English accepted an offer of support tendered by the President and Trustees of Indiana University.

In July 1959 Ashton's title and responsibilities again were changed when he became Vice-President for Graduate Development. He held this position, along with that of Dean of the Graduate School, until January 1965, at which time he took a leave of absence to become the first Director of the Graduate Academic Center Program of the United States Office of Education established under the Higher Education Facilities Act. (In October 1952 he was a member of the planning commission of the Conference on Higher Education held in Washington, D.C.)

John Ashton's work on Old English ballads was widely published in literary journals, and he served as Review Editor of the Journal of American Folklore. He also served as an international research fellow at Huntington Library in California (1932–33).

In retirement, Ashton was writing a history of university activities for the Indiana University sesquicentennial celebration when he died on November 8, 1971, in his office in the Indiana Memorial Union to which he had just walked from his home about a mile away. Mrs. Ashton had preceded him in death in November, 1969. He was survived by his two daughters and eight grandchildren.

Ashton was a member of the Modern Language Association, America Folklore Society (and it's representative for three years, beginning in 1962, to the American Council of Learned Societies); National Council of Teachers of English, The Facsimile Text Society, Delta Sigma Rho, a debating fraternity; and Phi Beta Kappa, which elected him to membership in the Phi Beta Kappa Association. He was active in the Episcopal Church and in 1952 was one of two lay members appointed to the Joint Liturgical Commission of the Episcopal Church for a six-year term.

When Ashton returned to IU in the summer of 1966, he resumed his teaching with a professorship of English and

Folklore. He retired on July 1, 1970, with the title of Professor Emeritus of English and Folklore. That same year the IU Chapter of Sigma Delta Chi journalism society presented its Rocking Chair award for his outstanding service to the University.

Thaddeus M. Bonus, 1931–
VICE-PRESIDENT, UNIVERSITY RELATIONS, 1976–1980

Thaddeus M. Bonus, journalist and communication specialist, son of Casimir Carroll and Marie (Kolodeis) Bonus, was born April 6, 1931, in Rochester, New York, where he attended secondary school and obtained a B.A. (1954) from the University of Rochester. Ted then obtained a M.S. (1955) from Columbia University. While at the University of Rochester he belonged to the Alpha Delta Phi social fraternity, participated in Interfraternity Council affairs, and was a member of the Varsity Golf Team. At Columbia, Ted was awarded an internship with the state senate. During his early college years (1952–54), he worked as a reporter for the *Democrat and Chronicle* in Rochester.

After graduating from Columbia, Ted entered the Military Services (1955–57) as editor of the *U.S. Army of the Pacific Newspaper*. Upon his discharge from the Army, Bonus was employed as Assistant Director of the News Bureau at the University of Pennsylvania (1958–61), from which he moved on to a variety of business experiences. He was a member of the Public Relations Staff, Eastman Kodak Company (1961–63), and Manager of Internal Communications, KMS Industries in Ann Arbor, Michigan (1967–70). He then returned to academia as Director of State and Community Relations at the University of Michigan (1970–75), and became Vice-President for University Relations at Indiana University in 1976.

Ted was a member of the Council for the Advancement and Support of Education (CASE), served on the University Relations Council of the National Association of State Universities and Land-Grant Colleges, and was a member of the Bloomington Chamber of Commerce. He also held member-

Thaddeus M. Bonus

ships in the Columbia Club (Indianapolis) and the Bloomington Country Club.

He resigned September 30, 1980, and currently (1982) is Director of Public Information at the University of North Carolina.

Samuel Edward Braden, 1914–
VICE-PRESIDENT, 1959–1967

Samuel Edward Braden, educator and economist, son of Samuel Ray and Mary Elizabeth (Altman) Braden, was born on June 6, 1914 in Hoihow, Hainan, China, where his parents were serving as Presbyterian missionaries. He graduated from high school in McAlester, Oklahoma (1929), having attended four high schools in three different states. He worked on a Kansas farm in the summers. Samuel obtained his A.B. (1932) from the University of Oklahoma where he was elected to Phi Eta Sigma (freshman scholarship society), Phi Beta Kappa, Beta Gamma Sigma (commerce scholarship society) and was a member of Sigma Alpha Epsilon social fraternity. Samuel went on to the University of Wisconsin where he obtained his M.A. (1935) and Ph.D. (1941).

While working on his Ph.D. at the University of Wisconsin he married Beth Black of Richland Center, Wisconsin, on June 19, 1937. At the same time Braden joined the Economics faculty of Indiana University as an instructor, working his way up to a full Professorship by 1955. The Bradens had four children: Mary Beth (Mrs. W. Richard West, Jr.), Stephen Black, John Black, and David Black. Mary Beth and Stephen graduated from the University of Michigan; John and David graduated from Miami (Ohio) University. All are Phi Beta Kappas. Mary Beth also took a law degree at Stanford University.

Samuel had a leave of absence from 1942 to 1946, during which time he served as Senior Economist of the Combined Raw Materials Board (1942–43) and then entered the United States Air Force as a private (1943), leaving as a First Lieutenant and Statistical Control Officer (1946).

Samuel Edward Braden

In 1949–50 Braden held a Fulbright Senior Research Fellowship. He spent the year studying and doing research at the London School of Economics.

In February 1954 he became Associate Dean of the College of Arts and Sciences and held this post until July 1959, when he became Vice-President and Dean for Undergraduate Development.

Braden was a prolific writer of economic journal articles and co-author of several books. He lectured frequently to widely diverse groups and was active in numerous organizations associated with education.

During his tenure as Vice-President, Braden traveled widely in Asia and South America in connection with Indiana University's overseas programs and as a representative of the Midwest Universities Consortium for International Activities, of which Indiana University is a member.

In May 1967 Braden resigned to accept the presidency of Illinois State University at Normal, Illinois in September of that year. He resigned this post in 1970 and returned to Indiana University as Professor of Economics and Chairman of the Division of Business and Economics at Indiana University/Southeast in New Albany, Indiana (1970–79). Since 1979 he held the title of Professor Emeritus of Economics at IU Southeast.

Sam has been a member of the American Finance Association (past Vice-President); American Economics Association; Midwest Economics Association; Society for International Development; American Association of University Professors; Council on International Educational Exchange (Chairman of Committee on Academic Programs Abroad; Chairman, Board of Directors, 1969–74; Executive Committee, 1974–80; Treasurer, 1976–80); Indiana Conference of Higher Education (Executive Director, 1960–67); Board of Overseers of St. Meinrad College (1965–67, 1970–; Chairman, 1976–79); and the Foundation Board, Metropolitan State University, Minnesota (1970–80). He also is on the Board of Directors of the E. H. Hughes Construction Company, Jeffersonville (1981–) and the Westminister Village Kentuckiana (President, 1981–).

He is a Presbyterian and declares himself as nonpartisan politically.

Herman Thompson Briscoe, 1893–1960
VICE-PRESIDENT, 1942–1959

Herman Thompson Briscoe, educator, was born at Shoals, Indiana, November 6, 1893, son of John S. G. and Alice (Thompson) Briscoe. He was graduated from the Shoals High School and entered Indiana University in June, 1912, graduating A.B. with high distinction in 1917. He interrupted his college course to teach in the Shoals High School. During the year 1917–1918 he was superintendent of schools in Shoals. In spite of his heavy work load, at IU he participated in debate as a member of Tau Kappa Alpha (oratory and debate fraternity). He also took part in the so-called Extension Debates, a series of public discussions held throughout Indiana. Herman's graduate work was interrupted by the first World War, in which he served (May, 1918–February, 1919) first as an infantry private and then as a member of the Officer Training Corps, 85th Division. He was transferred by the Army to the Hercules Powder Company as a research chemist in explosives (1918–1919), where a laboratory explosion nearly cost his life.

Before returning to Indiana University, Briscoe taught at Stark's Military Academy, was Austin Teaching Fellow at Harvard University (1919–1920), and an instructor at Colby College (1920–22). In 1922 he enrolled as a graduate student in Indiana University and received the A.M. degree in 1923 and the Ph.D. degree in 1924. During the years 1922–1924 he also served as an Instructor in Chemistry. He was an Assistant Professor of Chemistry (1924–1926), Associate Professor (1926–1928), and from mid-1928, Professor of Chemistry. On the retirement of Professor R. E. Lyons in 1938, Mr. Briscoe became Chairman of the Department of Chemistry (1938–1941).

Briscoe had been appointed Faculty Adviser to Dental Students in 1928 and served until 1943. In April, 1938, he was appointed Special Administrative Assistant to the President, in charge of the Student Guidance Program which soon stimu-

Herman Thompson Briscoe

lated the founding of the Junior Division (now the University Division). He was appointed Dean of the Faculties (1940–1942), in accordance with the Self-Survey Plan. He had been a member of the committee which developed this plan. He then served as Acting Dean of the School of Business, April 30, 1942, to October 5, 1942, when Dean Arther Weimer was called to active service. In July, 1942, Briscoe was appointed Vice-President of the University and Dean of Faculties (1942–59), and then served as consultant to the President (1959–60). At the time of his death he was serving as a consultant to the faculty committee appointed by the Board of Trustees to advise in the search for a successor to President Wells, whose retirement from office was to occur in 1962.

On September 15, 1928, Herman married Orah Cole whom he met when she was a student in his General Chemistry course. They had four children: Catherine Alice (Mrs. Stephen Ayres, A.B. 1962) Robert Herman (B.S., 1955); William Cole (A.B., 1961; M.D., 1966); and James Frederick (deceased August 10, 1944).

Dean Briscoe was appointed (1942) as a consultant to the Division of Professional and Technical Training, War Manpower Commission, Washington, D.C., and held the title of Chief of the Division from 1942 to 1944. Briscoe wrote widely in the field of chemistry, producing several textbooks which were periodically updated. He also was an editorial adviser to a publisher of a series of chemistry books.

He was active in both scientific and social organizations and held memberships in the American Chemical Society, Indiana Academy of Science, American Association for the Advancement of Science, Phi Beta Kappa, Sigma Xi (scientific research), Lambda Chi Alpha (social fraternity). Briscoe was known widely as an outstanding teacher and for many years was the only faculty member who had been the recipient of both the awards which Sigma Delta Chi gives annually—the Leather Medal (1942), for the person who has given the most distinguished service to the University, the Brown Derby (1939), for the most popular professor. He held memberships in the Kiwanis and the Masonic Order, was a Democrat, and attended the Methodist Church.

In June 1945 Briscoe suffered a paralyzing cerebral hemorrhage from which he slowly regained his ability to carry on his administrative duties. In 1953 he sold his Bloomington residence and bought a house in Sarasota, Florida. Through a special arrangement made by the Board of Trustees, Briscoe alternated periodic residence in Bloomington and in Florida. While in Bloomington he lived at the Indiana University Memorial Union.

At his retirement dinner in June, 1959, the Alumni Association presented Briscoe's portrait to the University. He suffered a heart attack in his office in September, 1960, and died on October 8, 1960, in Robert Long Hospital at the Indiana University Medical Center. A memorial service was held at Indiana University on October 11, 1960, the same day he was buried in Sarasota, Florida.

An endowed professorship in chemistry was established in his name and in September, 1965, a new undergraduate student residence was dedicated and named for Briscoe.

Byrum Earl Carter, Jr., 1922–
VICE-PRESIDENT, 1974–1975
Chancellor, Bloomington Campus, 1969–1974

Byrum E. Carter, political scientist and administrator, son of Byrum Earl and Myrtle Virginia (Madison) Carter, was born in Shawnee, Oklahoma, on March 22, 1922. He attended local schools through high school and then entered Tillman County Junior College in Frederick, Oklahoma (1939–41). Byrum obtained his B.A. from Oklahoma University (1943), where he was a member of the Congress Club, and Pi Sigma Alpha. He later attended the University of Wisconsin (1945–47) and received his Ph.D. there (1951).

He joined the Marine Corps (1943) but received a medical discharge within a year. He then worked for eight months as a wage-rate analyst in the Seventh Region War Labor Board.

Byrum married Beth Peter of Frederick, Oklahoma, on May 14, 1944. They had two children: Terry Elizabeth Hedrick

Byrum Earl Carter, Jr.

(B.A. 1971; U. of Missouri Ph.D. 1975) and Keith Madison (attended Ferris State University, Big Rapids, Michigan for two years and later attended Indiana University).

Carter joined the Indiana University faculty (1947) as an Instructor in the Department of Government (later the Political Science Department) and by 1960 had attained the rank of full Professor. Meantime Carter had assumed the half-time duty of Assistant Dean of Faculties (1959–61). He continued as Acting Assistant Dean (1961–62) and as Acting Associate Dean (1963) until he finally took over as Acting Chairman of the Department of Government (1963–64). He served as Dean of the College of Arts and Sciences (1966–69) and was appointed Chancellor of the Bloomington Campus (1969–74). As of July 1, 1974, Carter became the Vice President of the Bloomington Campus. In 1975 he took administrative leave (July 1, 1975– December 31, 1975) and then returned to teaching.

Byrum was the youngest person ever to receive the Fredric Bachman Lieber Award for distinguished teaching (1975). He has served as a member of the distinguished speakers panel of the Phi Beta Kappa Association, is a member of the American Political Science Association (Executive Council, 1962–64), and a member of the Midwest Conference of Political Scientists (Vice-President, 1975). The author of several books, Byrum has contributed articles to many professional journals in the field of political science.

Byrum is a voracious reader of wide-ranging tastes and a devotee of classical music, particularly the works of Bach. His other, more active, extra-curricular activities have included tennis, billiards, and golf, the latter having replaced his participation in tennis in more recent years. Carter also has a strong interest in football, which he enjoys in person as well as on television, with IU football never having quite replaced his allegiance to the University of Oklahoma's team. He and his wife are avid golfers.

Carter gives allegiance to the Democratic Party.

Ralph Leonard Collins

Ralph Leonard Collins 1907–1963
VICE-PRESIDENT, 1959–1963

Ralph Leonard Collins, scholar, educator and administrator, son of Leonard Alfred and Mae (Harrington) Collins, was born November 19, 1907, in Eclectic, Alabama. He attended Sidney Lanier high school in Montgomery, Alabama, and went on to get his A.B. in three years at the University of the South in Sewanee, Tennessee (1928), and his Ph.D. from Yale (1933). He became an Instructor at the University of Tennessee (1934–35) and joined the English faculty at Indiana University (1935). He taught modern drama and advanced to a full Professorship in 1953. Meanwhile Collins concurrently held the position of Assistant Dean of Faculties (1948–53) and Associate Dean of Faculties (1953–59), becoming Dean of Faculties and Vice-President in 1959.

On June 13, 1940, Ralph married Dorothy Ellen Craig, of Evansville, Indiana, and they had one son, David Harrington.

Collins was an active member of numerous general and departmental committees during his Indiana University career as well as Indiana University representative to a variety of national meetings of the Higher Education Division of NEA, Modern Language Association of America, American Council on Education, State University Association, and a commissioner and examiner for the North Central Association, the accrediting agency for Indiana and eighteen other states. In addition he was student hall headmaster, Director of the Indiana University Writer's Conference for eight years (1941–49), a widely-known critic and reviewer of theatre productions, a reader for Book-of-the-Month Club, and a critic and writer for both the *Atlantic Monthly* and scholarly journals in the field of literary criticism.

He was an enthusiastic follower of sports and served as a part-time coach for the varsity tennis team (1940–45). He was interested in civic affairs as well and served on the Bloomington Human Relations Commission.

Ralph was a member of Phi Beta Kappa, Modern Language Association, Kappa Sigma social fraternity, an honorary member of Beta Gamma Sigma, and a member of the Baptist

Church. He was a Commissioner and Examiner for the North Central Association and was elected in 1963 to a five-year term on the Association's executive board. In November 1962 Collins had been named to the newly created position of Executive Secretary of the Indiana Conference on Higher Education (composed of the Presidents of all Hoosier colleges and universities) and also was named Secretary-Treasurer. He also represented IU for ROTC and AFROTC at various military installation meetings in 1951–52.

Ralph Collins' untimely death at age fifty-five was due to a heart attack.

David Richard Derge, Jr., 1928–
EXECUTIVE VICE-PRESIDENT, 1968–1972

David Richard Derge, Jr., political scientist and educator, son of David Richard and Blanche (Butterfield) Derge, was born on October 10, 1928, in Kansas City, Missouri, where he attended school through high school. He went on to the University of Missouri and obtained an A.B. (1950). Northwestern University was his choice for the A.M. (1951) and Ph.D. (1955). During this period he took the school year of 1951–52 to serve as a teaching assistant at the University of Washington, returning to Northwestern University to hold the same type of position (1952–54). Dave enlisted in the United States Army (1946–48) and joined the United States Naval Reserve (1952), holding the rank of Commander when he retired (1973).

In 1951 he married Elizabeth Anne Greene (deceased May 1971), daughter of Mr. and Mrs. J. E. Greene of Mayfield, Kentucky, and they had two children: David Richard III (B. Music 1976) and Dorothy Anne. Dave married Patricia Jean Williams of Carthage, Illinois, on September 2, 1972, and they have two children: William David and Mary Jennifer.

After graduating from Northwestern University, Derge was an instructor at the University of Missouri (1954–56), before joining the faculty at Indiana University as an Assistant Pro-

David Richard Derge, Jr.

fessor (1956). He progressed through the academic ranks to a full professorship in 1965, in which year he also became Associate Dean of the Graduate School. In 1967, Dave exchanged his title for that of Associate Dean of Faculties, adding the title of Acting Director of the Bureau of Institutional Research in October 1968.

In December 1968 he was tapped as Executive Vice-President and Dean for Administration, which position he held until he resigned in January 1972 to become President of Southern Illinois University. While Executive Vice-President of Indiana University, Derge was Acting President during the illness of President Sutton in May and June 1969 and, again, from October 1970 to January 1971. Derge resigned from the presidency of Southern Illinois University in March 1974 to return to teaching in political science.

While at Indiana University Dave earned many honors including Sigma Delta Chi's Brown Derby (1962–63) and The Ulysses G. Weatherly Distinguished Teaching Award (1964). Dave also found time to be active in local government and was elected to a four-year term on the Bloomington City Council (1963); later (1964) the Indiana State Junior Chamber of Commerce chose him as one of Indiana's "Five Outstanding Young Men." In 1973 he received an honorary LL.D. from Hanyang University in Korea.

Derge had many federal government contacts and had served in many consultant capacities for various government agencies, primarily those related to higher and international education, such as the U.S. Advisory Commission for International Education and Cultural Affairs, a presidential advisory group (1969–76). He also served as a White House consultant (1968–71). In the latter capacity he directed the confidential public opinion polls for President Richard M. Nixon. He had been offered positions as Assistant Secretary of State, of the Air Force and of the Interior; Director of the Bureau of Census and Deputy Commissioner for Higher Education in Health, Education and Welfare. The latter position had been refused just before he accepted the presidency at Southern Illinois University. He then said he was severing all political ties because he didn't believe a university president should be involved in politics and because he hoped to devote the rest of his professional career to education.

Dave traveled widely to evaluate some of the technical assistance programs of Americans in foreign countries, including those operated by Indiana University. He has published extensively in this area of research. Derge also was widely known for his work in educational television, having served as a teacher for a recorded closed-circuit series in American Government at the Bloomington and regional campuses

Derge holds memberships in Phi Beta Kappa, Pi Sigma Alpha (national political science honorary), Alpha Pi Zeta, Kappa Sigma social fraternity, the Presbyterian Church, Bloomington Squash Racquets (former member), La Table Six, and the American Political Science Association.

Joseph Amos Franklin, 1904–1981
VICE-PRESIDENT AND TREASURER, 1948–1971
Treasurer, 1946–1948

Joseph Amos Franklin, administrator and fiscal officer, was born on a farm in Madison County, Indiana, on July 5, 1904, the son of Pierce and Emma Zetta (Williams) Franklin. He attended a country school and then entered the Markleville High School, where he was graduated in May, 1922. In the fall of 1922 he entered Indiana University, but an appendectomy, a few weeks later, from which recovery was slow, made it necessary to postpone the beginning of his university course until the fall of 1923. He was graduated in June, 1927, with the degree B.S. in Business.

During the year 1926–1927 he had been employed, on a part-time basis, as an accountant in the Bursar's Office. After his graduation, he began full-time work in that office, August 1, 1927, as audit clerk. During the seven years between 1927 and 1934, he was promoted to the position of accountant, and then chief accountant. When, in June 1936, the Office of Controller was created, Mr. Franklin became Assistant to the Controller. This title was changed to Assistant Controller, 1938–

Joseph Amos Franklin

1942. Effective as of July 1, 1942, Ward G. Biddle was appointed Vice-President and Treasurer, and Mr. Franklin's title became Assistant Treasurer, 1942–1946.

On the death of Treasurer Biddle, Franklin was appointed Treasurer, effective as of July 1, 1946. Two years later, June 10, 1948, he was given the full title of his predecessor, Vice-President and Treasurer of Indiana University, effective as of July 1, 1948.

On June 9, 1926, Franklin married Beatrice Long. They had four children: Zetta Ann (Mrs. Raymond Anderson, A.B. 1950, MAT 1963), Richard Paul (B.S. 1950), Janet (Mrs. Denny Carrell), and Joseph Arnold (B.S. 1959, J.D. 1963, M.B.A. 1965).

Joe made an inspection trip to Southeast Asia (1962) for IU in connection with various projects in which the University was involved in Pakistan, Thailand, and Indonesia. He made several trips to Peru in connection with a Ford Foundation project at San Marcos University to advise the officials there on methods of centralizing business procedures.

Franklin was active in many civic affairs in addition to those academic activities connected with the University. He was a life member of the Riley Board, a President of the Indiana Business Officer's Association, President (1966) of the Central Association of College and Business Officers, President of the Bloomington Lions Club, a trustee of the Lions Club Cancer Control Fund of Indiana, Vice-President of the Association of Universities for Research in Astronomy (1968), President of the Indiana Chapter of Myasthenia Gravis, Inc., and a member of the Heart Program-Project Committee of the National Heart Institute.

In 1958 the Franklins moved into Woodburn House as the official hosts for that residence after Dr. Herman B Wells moved to Bryan House, the official presidential residence. They remained in residence until 1968.

In 1971, after twenty-five years of service, Joe asked to be relieved of his duties as Vice-President and Treasurer. Upon his retirement he assumed the role of fiscal counsel to the University President until 1975.

In 1973 Franklin became the second person to receive the

E. Ross Bartley award for meritorious and extraordinary performance as an administrator. He also received the IU Distinguished Alumni Service Award (1976).

Joe was a very active member and elder of the Church of Christ. Politically he was an Independent: he always said he tried to vote for the best man for a given post.

He died in Bloomington Hospital on July 19, 1981, and was interred at Mechanicsburg, Indiana.

Kenneth R. R. Gros Louis, 1936–
Vice-President, 1980–

Kenneth Gros Louis, educator and administrator, son of Albert W. (of Blackstone, Massachusetts) and Jeannette E. (Richards) Gros Louis (of Woonsocket, Rhode Island), was born December 18, 1936, in Nashua, New Hampshire. He attended secondary schools in New England through Phillips Exeter Academy (1955). He received his B.A. from Columbia College (1959), where he was elected to Phi Beta Kappa, and received the Bjorkwald prize and the Columbia University Club Awards. He also became a member of Sigma Nu social fraternity (and held several different offices including that of Commander), served as President of the Residence Halls Association, and was a member of the Senior Society of Sachems. He also received his M.A. from Columbia (1960) and took his Ph.D. at the University of Wisconsin, (1964), where he had a summer fellowship (1962) and was a Knapp Fellow (1963–64).

On August 28, 1965, Ken married Dolores K. Winandy of Milwaukee, Wisconsin, who also has a Ph.D. from the University of Wisconsin (1968) and is an Associate Professor, part-time, in the Honors Division at Indiana University, Bloomington. They have two daughters: Amy Catherine (born 1967) and Julie Jeannette (born 1969).

Ken served as a teaching assistant (1960–63) at the University of Wisconsin and then joined the Indiana University faculty as an Assistant Professor of English and Comparative Literature (1964). He advanced through the academic ranks to

Kenneth R. R. Gros Louis

become a full Professor (1973), having served meanwhile as the Assistant Chairman of the Comparative Literature Program (1966). He received the Ulysses G. Weatherly Award for Distinguished Teaching (1970). Over the years, Gros Louis assumed more and more administrative responsibilities: Associate Dean, College of Arts and Sciences (1970); Chairman of the Department of English (1973); Dean of the College of Arts and Sciences (1978). He was chosen Vice-President of the Bloomington Campus (1980) to replace Vice-President Robert O'Neil who resigned to become President of the University of Wisconsin.

Almost immediately on becoming Vice-President for the Bloomington Campus, Gros Louis set up a toll-free phone line (a so-called hot line) whereby he could be reached every Thursday from 2:30 to 5:30 p.m. to answer questions relating to the University from any student or citizen. He felt that there should be close relations between the University and its many constituencies.

Gros Louis also has presided over and participated in innumerable committees relating to academic and administrative affairs on the campus as well as to outside professional organizations. He has published a considerable number of articles in literary journals and written several books, most recently one on the Bible as literature. In addition, Ken has served as review editor for the *Yearbook of Comparative and General Literature,* and as an editorial advisor to several publishing companies and university presses, including the Indiana University Press. He also has served as an external evaluator for English and Comparative Literature departments throughout the United States.

Gros Louis has been active in many professional organizations such as the American Comparative Literature Association; American Association of University Professors; Modern Language Association; Renaissance Club, Indiana University (President, 1967–68); Language and Literature Club, Indiana University (President, 1968–69); Arts and Sciences CIC Representative (1970–72); Advisory Panel, Indiana Arts Commission (1974–76); Board of Visitors, University of Louisville (1976–78); Indiana Committee for the Humanities

(Chairman, 1980–); the National Research Council's Commission on Human Resources (1979–); and the Conference on Christianity and Literature (Board of Directors, 1980–). He has received grants from several organizations, including the National Endowment for the Humanities.

He has been active in community activities such as the Community Progress Council and the United Way (1981–82 Campus Chairman). Ken holds membership in the Bloomington Rotary Club and Bloomington Swim Club. He is a Democrat and attends the Catholic Church.

Joseph Robert Hartley, 1931–
Vice-President, 1968–1972

Joseph Robert Hartley, educator and administrator, son of Alton Henry and Josephine Lucille (Norris) Hartley, was born June 25, 1931, in Portland, Indiana. He attended local schools through high school, at which he was valedictorian of his class (1949). After a year at Ball State Teachers College (1949–50), Joe attended Indiana University (B.S. in Business 1953 *cum laude*, M.B.A. 1954, D.B.A. 1957), achieving a 4.0 grade for all three degrees. At Indiana University Joe received the Earhart Fellowship (1955), two Welborn (1952 and 1953), two Little 500 (1952 and 1953), and four state scholarships (1949–53). He was an ROTC Cadet Colonel, and he received the Chicago Tribune Gold and Silver medals (1952 and 1953), the Beta Gamma Sigma Senior Scholarship Award (1953), the Alpha Kappa Psi Scholarship key (1953), and the Benjamin Franklin Award (1954).

On July 22, 1951 Joe married Louise Evelyn Logan of Portland (B.S. Education 1953), and they had three children: Karen Louise, Lynn Marie, and Greg.

Hartley worked and/or had fellowships and teaching assignments at Indiana University from 1951 until 1956, when he left to serve two years in the United States Air Force as Assistant to the Director of Transportation at the Air Force Logistic's Command Headquarters under General E. B. Cassady in Dayton, Ohio. In July 1957 he returned to Indiana

Joseph Robert Hartley

University as an Assistant Professor of Business Administration and continued to move up through the academic ranks until he became a full Professor (1963). Hartley added the administrative title of Associate Dean of Faculties (1965) and subsequently held the positions of Acting Director of the Bureau of Institutional Research (1968–73), Acting Dean of Faculties (November–December 1968), Vice-President and Dean of Faculties (December 1968–September 1969); and Vice-President and Dean for Academic Affairs (September 1969–March 1972). Joe resigned August 1973 to go to the University of Missouri as Chancellor but remained only a year. He left Missouri to become Vice President of the Citizen Bank of Portland, Indiana (1974–76), and then rejoined the IU faculty (1976).

With all of his administrative and teaching responsibilities Hartley found time to write and publish numerous books, monographs, and articles for professional journals and commercial business publications. Some of his publications resulted from research studies he directed on campus for the government and for private industry both at home and abroad. Hartley is an authority on transportation and finance and has served as a consultant for such organizations as the Chicago Board of Trade, Indiana Port Commission, American Waterways Operation Association, Trinity River Improvement Association, Tennessee-Tombigbee Waterway Development Authority, Harland Bartholomew Association, Arthur D. Little Company, Grocery Manufacturers Association, and some twenty-five business firms. He also served as a transport economist for the World Bank Magdalena Valley Planning Mission in Colombia, South America (1959); for the Brookings Institution in Colombia, South America (1964); and as an educational consultant to the University of Pittsburgh for the Ford Foundation (1966); and under a Ford Foundation Grant to Islamabad University in Pakistan (1967).

Hartley also has conducted a study of potential economic development in the Wabash River drainage basin for the Wabash Interstate Commission of Illinois and Indiana (1976). He was part-time Director of Indiana Railroad Planning for the Federal Railroad Administration (1977–80), a member of the President's National Waterways Study Commission (1980-82), and is currently (1982) conducting a study of investment strategy for financial institutions. He has delivered innumerable speeches to professional groups and has been called as an expert witness on some thirty occasions by committees of the U.S. Senate, House of Representatives, Interstate Commerce Commission and the Indiana Public Service Commission.

Joe serves on the Board of Directors of the Bloomington National Bank (1973-) and that of Zenith Laboratories in New York City (1976-).

Among the various honors that have come to Hartley are the following: School of Business Distinguished Teaching Award (1964), DBA Association Distinguished Teaching Award (1982), Indiana Academy of Science Distinguished Service Award (1981), and five research fellowships.

He holds memberships in the American Economic Association, American Management Association, Regional Science Association, Society for International Development, American Society of Traffic and Transportation, Phi Beta Kappa, Beta Gamma Sigma (business scholastic fraternity), Alpha Kappa Psi (which he served as President), Columbia Club, Bloomington Country Club, St. Louis Club, Portland Country Club, Bloomington Rotary, and Portland Lions; he is a Methodist and a Republican.

Ray Lorenzo Heffner, Jr., 1925–
VICE-PRESIDENT, 1964–1966

Ray Lorenzo Heffner, educator and administrator, son of Ray Lorenzo and Gladys (Gordy) Heffner (both of whom were in the field of education), was born in Durham, North Carolina, on March 7, 1925. He spent part of his boyhood in Baltimore, and his family later moved to Seattle, Washington, where he graduated from Broadway High School in 1941. Before finishing his B.A., Ray served in the United States Naval Reserve (1943–46) on active duty as a Seebee in the Pacific. He later

Ray Lorenzo Heffner, Jr.

was commissioned as an officer in Naval Intelligence and received Japanese-language training at Oklahoma State University. His college work was taken at Yale University, where he received a B.A. (1948), M.A. (1950), and Ph.D. (1953).

On June 16, 1951 Ray married Ruth Adele Cline of Paris, Kentucky, and they had two sons: David (born 1959) and Christopher (born 1961).

Heffner was an instructor in English at the University of Kentucky (1950–51) prior to joining the Indiana University English Department in 1953. He moved up the academic ladder to become Associate Professor of English (1960). Meanwhile he also assumed the position of Assistant Dean of Faculties (1959), becoming Associate Dean in 1962. He spent a year at the British Museum in London (February 1960–January 1961) doing Shakespearean research on a Guggenheim Fellowship. In January 1963 Heffner resigned to become Vice-President of the University of Iowa. He returned to Indiana University in July 1964 to become Vice-President and Dean of Faculties, and was Acting Dean of the Graduate School (February to June 1965). During his tenure as Vice-President at IU, Heffner served as a member of the U.S. Surgeon General's Council on Nursing Training. Heffner again resigned from Indiana University (June 1966) to serve as President of Brown University. He moved on to become the Provost of the University of Iowa (1969–73). He currently (1982) is Professor of English at the University of Iowa.

While at Indiana University, Heffner served as chairman of the Vice-President's Committee of Indiana's four state universities; he was active as a consultant and examiner in the North Central Association of Colleges and Secondary Schools; he had much to do with establishing Indiana University's first honors program for undergraduates and was the Indiana University representative on the Committee on Institutional Cooperation (composed of Big Ten Universities and the University of Chicago).

Heffner also holds honorary degrees from Franklin College (Litt. D. 1966), University of Rhode Island (LL.D. 1967), Bryant College (DBA 1967). Other honors he has received include Phi Beta Kappa, Guggenheim Fellowship (1960), Sterling Fellowship (1952), and the Sigma Delta Chi Leather Medal (1966) for outstanding contributions to Indiana University.

Ray is a member of the Modern Language Association of America, Renaissance Society of America, and the Shakespeare Association of America.

Glenn Ward Irwin, Jr., 1920–
Vice-President, 1973–

Glenn Ward Irwin, Jr., physician and educator, son of Glenn Ward (of Rochdale, Indiana) and Elsie Browning Irwin (of Greencastle, Indiana), was born in Rochdale, Indiana, on July 18, 1920. He graduated from Rochdale high school (1938) and then attended Indiana University, where he earned a B.S. (1942) and M.D. (1944). Glenn did his internship at Methodist Hospital and a residency at Indiana University Medical Center before his Army service (Captain, M.C., A.U.S., 1946–48; Chief of Medicine, Schofield Barracks General Hospital, 1946–48). He became a Diplomate of the America Board of Internal Medicine and a Fellow of the American College of Physicians (1952). He was Governor of the American College of Physicians for Indiana (1964–70).

On December 26, 1943, Glenn married Marianna Ashby (A.B. 1943), and they had three children: Ann (Mrs. John Warden, A.B. 1971); William (Bradley University, B.S. 1972); Elizabeth (Mrs. Gary A. Schiffli, A.B. 1977, M.A. 1979).

Dr. Irwin joined the Indiana University faculty in 1950 as an instructor in medicine and assumed increasingly more responsible posts as he moved up to full professor (1961). He became Dean of the Indiana University Medical School (1965), where he established a reputation as an outstanding educator; he became Chancellor (1973) of Indiana University/Purdue University at Indianapolis (Indiana University and Purdue University at Indianapolis having been merged in 1969); and finally Vice-President of Indiana University at Indianapolis (1974).

Glenn Ward Irwin, Jr.

Irwin has been instrumental in developing an innovative statewide system for medical education in Indiana, in cooperation with other institutions of higher education. He has published a number of articles in professional journals, holds board membership in a number of civic and professional organizations, and has been a member of the Governor's Commission on Medical Education.

Irwin is a member of the American Medical Association, American College of Physicians, Indiana State Medical Association, Association of American Medical Colleges, Indiana Society of Chicago, Riley Memorial Association, Contemporary Club of Indianapolis, Rotary, 500 Festival Association, Indianapolis Literary Society, Columbia Club, Meridian Hills Country Club, Scottish Rite of Indianapolis (33rd degree), and the Presbyterian Church.

He also belongs to the honorary fraternities of Alpha Omega Alpha, Sigma Xi, and Beta Gamma Sigma, and received the Distinguished Alumnus Award from Indiana University Medical School (1972).

J. Gus Liebenow, 1925–
VICE-PRESIDENT, 1973–1974
Acting Vice-President, 1972–1973

J. Gus Liebenow, son of J. Gus, Sr., and E. Louise Leahy Liebenow, was born on May 4, 1925, in Berwyn, Illinois, where he attended school through high school. He then entered the University of Chicago, but his studies were interrupted by World War II. He was a Staff Sergeant in the United States Army Medical Corp (1943–46), serving in both European and Pacific theatres. He resumed his studies at the University of Illinois and received the B.A. *summa cum laude* (1949) and M.S. (1950). He was elected to Phi Beta Kappa and Phi Kappa Phi (scholarship honoraries). Liebenow was a Goodwin Fellow at Harvard University (1951–52) and then returned to the midwest, where he obtained his Ph.D. in Political Science at Northwestern University (1955). He held several

J. Gus Liebenow

fellowships during his university years: Illinois (1949–50), Harvard (Ozia Goodwin Memorial 1951–52), Northwestern (1954–55), Social Science Research Fellow for East African Research (1953–54), and Ford Foundation Foreign Area Fellow (1954–56).

On August 2, 1956, Gus married Beverly J. Bellis of Berwyn, Illinois, in London, England. They had four children: B. Diane (Mrs. George Gray, B.S. 1968, M.S. 1969, special degree in audio-visual communications 1975), Debra Lynn (Mrs. John Daly, B.A. 1973), Jay Stanton (B.S. 1982), and John Stuart.

Before joining the Indiana University faculty (1958), Liebenow was a Teaching Associate (1952–53) and Research Associate (1954–55) at Northwestern University and Assistant Professor at the University of Texas (1956–58). He achieved full professorship (1963) and also served as the first Director of African Studies (1961–72), as well as holding the dual appointments of Dean for International Programs and Associate Dean for Research and Advanced Studies (1970–72). Liebenow was Acting Vice-President and Dean for Academic Affairs (1972–73), and then Vice-President and Dean for Academic Affairs (1973–1974).

He is a prolific writer and has published many articles and several books. He also is active in various university organizations, such as the University and Bloomington Faculty Councils (Secretary, 1976–77), member of Graduate Council, AAUP (President, Bloomington Chapter, 1979–80), and has served on numerous committees. Gus also has been a consultant to a number of government agencies (Peace Corps, Department of State, House Committee on Foreign Affairs, and U.S. Department of Education) focusing on various aspects of education. He has traveled widely, done research at educational institutions in many foreign countries, and has worked with UNESCO in Mexico on a basic education project. He also has been a consultant for a number of university presses.

Liebenow is a member of the African Studies Association (one of the thirty-seven Founding Fellows, 1957–58; Executive Board, 1964–67; Vice-President, 1976–77; President, 1977–78); International African Institute, London (Executive Council, 1977–, a member of the Governing Body, representing Indiana University, 1964–); American Political Science Association, Southern Political Science Association (Chairman of Membership Committee, 1956–58; member of Editorial Board, 1968–); Midwest Political Science Association (Executive Board, 1962–65); University Field Staff International (Faculty Associate, 1980–). He represented Indiana University at the Indiana Higher Education Telecommunications System (1972–74), Midwest Universities Consortium for International Activities (1971–74), and the Committee on Institutional Cooperation (1972–74).*

Liebenow holds memberships in Rotary International, Friends of Music (Life Member), Friends of Art, Audubon Society (Sassafras Chapter), Theatre Circle, Smithsonian Institute, African-American Institute, and is a life member of the Indiana University Alumni Association.

When he relinquished the Vice-Presidency (1974) he returned to full-time teaching as a Professor of Political Science.

Lynne Lionel Merritt, Jr., 1915–
Vice-President, 1965–1975

Lynne Lionel Merritt, Jr., research chemist and administrator, son of Lynne Lionel and Pauline (Brown) Merritt, was born September 10, 1915, in Alba, Pennsylvania. He attended school in various parts of the east, finally graduating from Radford High School in Detroit (1932). He went to Wayne State University in Detroit, where he obtained his B.S. (1936) and M.S. (1937). Lynne went on to take his Ph.D. (1940) at the University of Michigan.

Meanwhile, he married Lucille Elizabeth Widman on December 18, 1937, daughter of Mr. and Mrs. O. W. Widman of Detroit, Michigan. They had four children: Margaret (Mrs. David H. Bowen, B.S. in Education 1961), Lucille (Mrs. I. Clay Williams, B.S. in Medical Technology 1967, M.S. in Education

---

*The Committee on Institutional Cooperation consists of Big Ten Universities and the University of Chicago.

Lynne Lionel Merritt, Jr.

1973), Lynn R. (B.S. Purdue 1967, deceased) and Linda (Mrs. David Marler, B.S. in Medical Technology 1973, M.S. in Education 1978).

Lynne taught chemistry at Wayne State University and the University of Michigan from 1936 to 1942, before joining Indiana University as Assistant Professor of Chemistry in September 1942. He spent a 1949 sabbatical at the California Institute of Technology learning the x-ray diffraction method of crystal structure determinations. Returning to IU, he became active in the creation of the University's Research Computing Center and served as its Director (1952–55, 1958–59). He had progressed to full professor by 1953 and continued to assume ever more important administrative positions in research and academia, finally becoming Vice-President for Research and Dean for Advanced Studies (1965). The title of this position was changed (1966) to Vice-President and Dean, Research and Advanced Studies. Lynne held this position until 1975, when he became Special Assistant to the President, and Dean for Research Coordination and Development. In 1981 he returned to teaching chemistry, but retained the title of Special Assistant to the President for certain specialized research coordination functions.

Merritt has published innumerable research papers in scholarly journals and has represented Indiana University on many advisory committees in university and professional organizations, both domestic and international. He has been active in the development of electronic instruments for rapid chemical analysis, and devices produced by Merritt and his associates have proved highly efficient for the analysis of alloys and ores.

Lynne holds memberships in Alpha Chi Sigma, American Chemical Society (alternate councilor, 1948; chairman, local section, 1952–53), American Crystallographic Association, American Association for Advancement of Science (Fellow), American Institute of Chemists (Fellow), Gamma Alpha, Phi Kappa Phi, Phi Lambda Upsilon, Phi Beta Kappa (secretary, local chapter, 1959–61; President, 1964–65), Sigma Xi (President, local chapter, 1959–60), Indiana Academy of Science (Fellow), and the Society for International Development. He was a Guggenheim Fellow at California Institute of Technology (1955–56), a Fulbright Fellow in Paris (1963), and received the Distinguished Alumni Award from Wayne State University (1959). He also is President and Director of the Indiana Instrument and Chemical Corporation (1959–   ).

Merritt has traveled widely in Asia, Europe, South America, and Africa since International Programs reported to his office (1965–75), and has represented IU on the Board of Directors of the Midwest Universities Consortium for International Activities (1967–, Chairman, 1971–), Universities Space Research Association, and Associated Universities for Research in Astronomy (1982–). He edits the Association of IU Chemists Newsletter.

Lynne is an avid gardener, but finds time for golf, swimming, and sailing. He belongs to the Methodist Church and is a Republican.

Robert M. O'Neil, 1934–
Vice-President, 1975–1980

Robert M. O'Neil, lawyer and educator, son of Walter George and Isabel Sophia (Marchant) O'Neil, was born October 16, 1934, in Boston. He attended primary school in Winchester and Cambridge, Massachusetts, spent the years from 1949 to 1952 at Milton Academy in Milton, Massachusetts, and entered Harvard, where he obtained his A.B. (1956), and A.M. in American History (1957), and finally an LL.B. (1961).

During his Harvard days, Bob was on the photographic staff of the school newspaper and was a member of the debating team (and its President, 1955–1956). He was a member of Phoenix-SK Club (1954–1956) and the Hasty Pudding Society (1953–1956), and in the fall of his senior year, was elected to Phi Beta Kappa. He continues his interest in photography to this day. At the same time, between 1956–1961, he also served as an instructor in speech at Tufts University and at San Francisco College (1962).

While serving as a teaching fellow in American History (1961–1962), Bob did graduate work in law and then became

Robert M. O'Neil

a law clerk for Supreme Court Justice William J. Brennan, Jr. He subsequently wrote a number of legal articles and sections of books based on his Supreme Court experience.

From 1963–1967 O'Neil taught law at the University of California at Berkeley. He left California to become an assistant to Martin Meyerson, at the latter's request, when he took over as President of SUNY/Buffalo. At SUNY, a meeting with Warren Bennis eventually led O'Neil back to Berkeley in 1969, when Bennis was named President of that institution. He followed Bennis again in 1971, when the latter moved to Cincinnati, where Bob became Vice-President and Provost for Academic Affairs at the University of Cincinnati, and also taught law. O'Neil then moved up to Executive Vice-President for Academic Affairs (1972), which position he held when he came to Indiana University (1975).

Bob married Karen Elson of Chicago in June 18, 1967, and they had four children: Elizabeth (born 1968), Peter (born 1971), David (born 1973), and Benjamin (born 1977). The O'Neils, in spite of Bob's heavy schedule, maintain a strong family life. They play tennis and enjoy taking their children for walks. Bob wrestles with the children and reads to them nightly—and collects antique automobiles!

O'Neil has represented the university at many national and international meetings including a symposium in Kiel, Germany (March 1978); and has been a member of numerous AAU, NASULGC, and Law Association Committees.

In November 1978 he was named to a four-year term as a Trustee of Carnegie Foundation for the Advancement of Teaching. He was the only administrator in the country asked to serve on the Academic Freedom Governing Board of the American Association of University Professors (1970–72).

June 1980 saw the departure of the O'Neils for the University of Wisconsin, where Bob was inaugurated as President in September 1980.

William George Pinnell

William George Pinnell, 1922–
EXECUTIVE VICE-PRESIDENT, 1974–
Treasurer, 1971–1974

William George Pinnell, educator and administrator, son of George Mason and Anna (Wagner) Pinnell, was born in Clarksburg, West Virginia, on September 6, 1922. He attended local schools through high school, served in the Navy as an aviator (1942–47), and then entered West Virginia University, where he obtained his A.B. (1950) and M.A. (1952). He came to Indiana University for his D.B.A. (1954). His thesis was a comprehensive report which provided the facts needed for community planning in Evansville. At Indiana, George was a member of Acacia, Alpha Kappa Psi (business fraternity), Sigma Iota Epsilon (management-recognition society), Beta Gamma Sigma (business honorary), and Eta Alpha Psi (accounting honorary).

George, as he is better known, married Dorothy E. Graham on June 25, 1946, and they had a daughter, Georgia Graham (Mrs. Ronald F. Stowe, A.B. 1969).

Pinnell served as Research Assistant in the Bureau of Business Research, West Virginia University (1950–51). When he came to Indiana University to work on his D.B.A., he served as Assistant to the Dean of the Business School (1952–54). Upon obtaining his doctorate he was appointed Assistant Professor of Real Estate (1954–56) and Assistant Dean. George became Associate Professor of Real Estate (1956–61) and the same year was named Associate Dean of the Business School (1956–63). He served as Acting Dean (1959–60) when Dean Arthur Weimer was on sabbatical leave, and then Dean (1963–1971). Meanwhile he had advanced to the rank of full Professor (1961). In August 1971, when Joseph A. Franklin retired as Vice-President and Treasurer of Indiana University, the Trustees appointed Pinnell to replace Franklin as Treasurer (September 1, 1971–74). He became Executive Vice-President in 1974.

George has been called on to serve in many civic, state, and federal capacities along with his University duties. Governor Matthew Welsh appointed him to the fifteen-man Governor's

Manpower Advisory Committee (1959) to work with the Indiana Employment Security Division and the State Division of Vocational Education to help local training and retraining programs. He served on President-elect John Kennedy's Committee on Area Redevelopment (1960) and then was appointed to two subcommittees: one on Area Redevelopment headed by Senator Paul Douglas, and the other on Special Problems of the Labor Force headed by William L. Batt, Jr., Secretary of Labor and Industry in Pennsylvania. George was the research director of the Indiana Post-High School Study Commission (created by the 1961 Indiana General Assembly), for a study that recommended a plan for higher education, which has been largely adopted by the State, including the establishment of technical schools (Indiana Vocational Technical College).

Pinnell was elected to the Board of Directors of the Council for International Progress in Management (1964) for a three-year term. He also is on the Board of Directors of The Kroger Company (1966–), Central Soya Company, Inc. (1979–), Public Service Indiana (1979–), American Fletcher Mortgage Investors (1970–81), Indiana University Foundation, and has served as Vice-President of the Great Lakes States Industrial Development Council (1963–64). He has participated in such activities as the Young Presidents' Organization (1966) which holds week-long, seminar-type meetings to exchange ideas on mutual business problems, stressing educational benefits. He has also been cited as a "good neighbor" by Crane Naval Ammunition Depot for his efforts to revise the Business School curriculum to enable Crane employees to further their education in night courses. From 1967 to 1971 he was a member of the Air Force Institute of Technology Advisory Committee. He serves as President of the Monroe County Hospital Authority (1981–). He is the author of two books, has contributed a number of articles to professional journals, and has served on the Editorial Board of *Business Horizons.*

George holds memberships in the American Economic Association, American Finance Association, Indiana Academy of Social Sciences, Indiana University and West Virginia Alumni Associations, Friends of Music, Friends of Art, the

Well House Society, Bloomington Country Club, Metropolitan Club (New York City), Columbia Club, and the Elks. He belongs to the Methodist Church and is politically an Independent.

On March 1, 1983, he assumed the Presidency of the Indiana University Foundation. He retains his title of Executive Vice-President with some reduction of responsibilities in the latter area.

John William Snyder, 1924–
VICE-PRESIDENT, 1967–1969

John William Snyder, historian and specialist in the early civilization of Babylon and other Near Eastern countries, son of Walter A. and Bernice (Hibbs) Snyder, was born in Denver, Colorado, on February 18, 1924. He moved to California during his early years and graduated from Antelope Valley Joint Union High School in Lancaster, California. He did his college work at the University of Minnesota, receiving a B.A. (1950), M.A. (1952) and Ph.D. (1954). Meanwhile, in 1951, he took a B.D. at Northwestern Theological Seminary, also in Minneapolis.

Snyder served in the Army from February 1943 to February 1946, both in the United States and Germany, attaining the rank of Sergeant by the time he was discharged.

On July 10, 1946, John married Margaret Ann Heetderks, daughter of Dr. Bernard and Kathryn (Corlett) Heetderks of Boseman, Montana, and they had two children: Mark Alan and Kathryn Dee. Mark attended a program for high school students given in German at Indiana University (1968).

Snyder joined Indiana University in 1956 as an Assistant Professor of History and progressively worked his way up to a full professorship (1964). During the same year he became Associate Dean of Arts and Sciences. The following year he became Dean of the Junior Division, where he served until the summer of 1967, when he became Vice-President and Dean for Undergraduate Development. He concurrently held the post of Acting Chancellor from January to June 1969, when

John William Snyder

he resigned to accept the presidency of Westmont College in Santa Barbara, California. During the troubled period of the early months of 1969, John proved himself to be an outstanding mediator and administrator in handling of the student protests against fee increases.

During his tenure at Indiana University, Snyder took a sabbatical in the 1962–63 school year to do research on Alexander the Great for a book he was writing. He was elected an honorary fellow of the American Schools of Oriental Research at Baghdad, Iraq, which supervised the archeological activities of Americans in Iraq. He is the author of numerous articles published in scholarly journals and has written several books.

John was a member of Phi Beta Kappa, American Institute of Archeology (Secretary, 1958; President, 1959 of the Central Indiana Chapter), and the American Historical Association. At various times he belonged to either the Baptist or the Presbyterian Church. He was a Republican.

Snyder also served as a member of the Board of the President's Associates at Bethel College and Seminary (1968–70), Indiana State Scholarship Commission (1967–69), and Midwestern Regional Committee for Marshall Scholarships (1968–69).

Snyder became Executive Vice-Chancellor of the University of California at Santa Barbara (1970–1974) and then moved on to be Executive Vice-President and Provost of Kent State University at Kent, Ohio (1974–78). He stepped down from his administrative post to return to full-time teaching of history.

Edgar Gene Williams, 1922–
VICE-PRESIDENT FOR ADMINISTRATION, 1973–

Edgar Gene Williams, management expert, educator and administrator, son of N. Wesley and Anna L. (Wilsey) Williams, was born in Poseyville, Indiana, on May 4, 1922. He attended school through high school in Poseyville and entered Evansville College in 1940, where he won three letters in basketball and one in football. In 1941 he enlisted in the Army

Edgar Gene Williams

Reserves Corps and was placed on inactive duty, but was called up in 1943 as a Private in the Army Medical Corps. In December 1943 Williams graduated from the Medical Administrative Corps, OCS, at Camp Berkeley, Texas, as a Second Lieutenant. He served both in the States and in the European Theatre. Leaving the service on August 6, 1946, as a First Lieutenant, he returned to Evansville College, obtained his degree in Economics and Political Science (A.B. 1947), and was elected to Pi Gamma Mu (a national social science honorary).

Meanwhile Ed had married Joyce E. Grigsby, also of Poseyville, daughter of Melborn and Mildred (Sutton) Grigsby on May 7, 1944. They had two children: Cynthia Ellen (Mrs. Mahigian Smith, A.B. Litt. 1971) and Thomas Gene (B.S. Liberal Studies 1981).

Williams went on to obtain an MBA (1948) and a DBA (1952) from Indiana University, and then did post-doctoral research at Harvard and Stanford Universities in 1969–1970. While attending Indiana University, Williams was a graduate assistant in management. He became an Instructor (1948) and moved up through the ranks to full Professor (1960). From 1960 to 1965 Ed served as Chairman of the Organizational Behavior Area. He was appointed as the Associate Dean for Administration, from which post he also served as liaison to programs in East Pakistan, Yugoslavia, and Thailand. He also served as the faculty advisor for the Indiana Student Chapter of the Society for the Advancement of Management. Retaining his position as Professor of Business Administration, he chaired the President's University Task Force on Management and Organization in 1971 and became the Executive Assistant to the President in 1972, moving up to Vice-President for Administration in 1974.

Williams has been a consultant for numerous companies over the years in the United States and abroad. He holds memberships in the American Management Association, Academy of Management, American Society for Personnel Administration, and the Indiana Academy of Social Science. He is an honorary key holder of the Graduate School of Savings and Loan, a member of Beta Gamma Sigma (business honorary) and Sigma Iota Epsilon (management honorary).

He received the Alumni Excellence Award from the University of Evansville (1974) and is the author of several articles, monographs, and books in the areas of personnel and general management.

Ed is a Mason and member of the Scottish Rite, Optimist Club, Bloomington Chamber of Commerce, and the Indianapolis Athletic Club. He is an avid fisherman who guards the location of his favorite spots. He enjoys reading and golf, and continues his strong interest in sports, by serving as the liaison between the administration and the Intercollegiate Athletic Department.

Wendell William Wright, 1893–1961
VICE-PRESIDENT, 1952–1959

Wendell William Wright, son of Perry Wright and Anne Elizabeth (Talbott) Wright, was born December 27, 1893, in Greencastle, Indiana. He attended school through high school in Greencastle and then entered Indiana State Teachers College (ISTC) from which he obtained the AB (1916). He taught in rural schools (1914–1916), and upon graduating from ISTC he became the Principal of the Rockville, Indiana, high school until 1919, although he took time out in 1918 to serve as a Sergeant in the U.S. Army. He was a teacher and researcher at Arsenal Technology Schools in Indianapolis (1919–1924). During this period he went to the University of Chicago in summers to take graduate work and finally obtained his Ph.D. from Teachers College at Columbia University (1925).

In June 1922 Wright married Alita Lois Bussard of Milwaukee, Wisconsin (born November 15, 1890 in Black Earth, Wisconsin), who died in 1957. They had two children: Jean Talbott (Mrs. Carl Hammond) and Elizabeth Anne (Mrs. Andrew Petach). In March 1959 he married Wallace Montague, who had been principal of the J. K. Lilly Senior High School in Indianapolis.

Wendell joined the Indiana University School of Education

Wendell William Wright

(1925) as an Assistant Professor and over the years held increasingly more important positions including Dean of Elementary Education, Dean of Junior Division, Director of the Office of Veteran Affairs, Director of the Division of Research and Field Services, Director of Administrative Studies and Institutional Relations. He finally became Vice-President of Administrative Studies and Institutional Relations in January 1952, a post he held until June 1959.

He was a Phi Delta Kappa, a Mason, a Methodist, and held memberships in the Columbia Club (Indianapolis), Bloomington Country Club, American Education Research Assocation, Horace Mann League, National Research Association, and National Education Association.

In December 1950 Wright represented Indiana University as one of forty Americans attending the first World Conference of Universities in Nice, France. When he stepped down as an administrator in June, 1959, Wright went to Thailand to review and report on the School of Education program there. He was the author or co-author of a number of books on educational subjects and methods.

Wendell W. Wright died October 15, 1961, in Robert Long Hospital.

Chancellors

Victor Morton Bogle

Victor Morton Bogle, 1921–
CHANCELLOR, IU AT KOKOMO, 1969–1979

Victor Morton Bogle, historian and administrator, son of Elroy and Anna May (Black) Bogle, who were natives of Washington County, was born in New Albany on September 24, 1921. He attended local schools, graduating from New Albany High School, and took his A.B. at Indiana Central College (1947), where he was elected to the honor society Epsilon Alpha Alpha. Boston University was Victor's choice for his A.M. (1948) and his Ph.D. (1951), after which he taught American History one summer at Northwestern University before entering the U.S. Air Force Intelligence (1952) as a research analyst. He left the Air Force (August 1954) for an appointment as Associate Professor of History with Tougaloo Southern Christian College in Tougaloo, Mississippi (September 1954–57).

On March 4, 1952, Bogle married Fern Jewell Schenk, and they had two daughters: Heather (B.SW. 1977) and April (a junior in 1982).

Bogle joined the Indiana University faculty (1957) as an Instructor in History and an Academic Counselor and was promoted through the ranks to Professor (1972). Meanwhile, he also assumed the various administrative roles of Director of Kokomo Campus, Assistant Dean of the Division of University Extension, and, finally, Chancellor of Indiana University at Kokomo, when the Extension Center became a regional campus.

During Bogle's administration the change in mission from an extension center to a regional campus required the building of a resident teaching facility as well as a new physical plant. Bogle also developed Project Outreach, by which students could obtain Indiana University credit through off-campus services. To further his knowledge in this area, Victor took a sabbatical to study planning models at Claremont (California) Graduate School (1969).

Bogle's interests extended to regional organizations, and he was elected to the Commission on Institutes of Higher Education of the North Central Association of Colleges and Schools

(1978–1981). He has served as a member of the Board of Directors of the Mental Health Association of Indiana, Incorporated (1980–1982), and the Indiana Central Alumni Association (1971–1973). Civic duties were also important to Bogle, and he served on the Chamber of Commerce Board of Directors (1967), the Symphonette Advisory Board, and the Kokomo Human Relations Committee (1966–1967). He is a member of the Board of Directors of the Opportunities Industrialization Center (1976–), the Howard County Mental Health Association (1973–1982); President, 1975), Kokomo Rotary and Elks.

Bogle holds memberships in the Pi Gamma Mu social science honorary, the Organization of American Historians, Mississippi Valley Historical Society, Indiana History Society, and Indiana Academic Scientists. He has contributed many articles to history journals. Victor is interested in major spectator sports and admits to playing "a poor game of tennis." He is a member of the Evangelical United Brethren Church and a Democrat.

He resigned as Chancellor in June 1979 to return to teaching.

Sylvia Edmonia Bowman, 1914–
Chancellor, Regional Campuses, 1972–75

Sylvia Edmonia Bowman, educator, writer, and lecturer, daughter of Clarence Steptoe and Alice M. (Smith) Bowman, was born in Advance, Indiana, on June 19, 1914, where she attended school through high school (1931). She attended Blackburn College (1933–34), obtained a B.S. from Central Normal College in Danville, Indiana (1939), an M.A. from the University of Chicago (1943), and was awarded a doctorate with very highest honors from the Sorbonne, University of Paris (1952).

At various periods Sylvia taught at Jamestown Elementary School (1935–41), taught English at Forest Park Junior High in Fort Wayne (1941–43), was Director of Publications, North Side High School, in Fort Wayne (1944–47), and was State

Sylvia Edmonia Bowman

Editor of the Fort Wayne *News-Sentinal* (1944). She continued to review books for the *News-Sentinal* and the *Chicago Tribune*.

Bowman joined the Fort Wayne Center as an Instructor in English (1947–53) and worked up the academic ladder to full Professor (1963), serving as Assistant Chairman of the Department of English at Fort Wayne (1965–71), and then Chairman of the Freshman Division of Arts and Sciences, as well as Acting Chairman of the Department of English (1970–72), before becoming Chancellor for Regional Campuses (1972–74). To the Chancellorship was added the duty of Coordinator of Academic Programs (1974–75). After Sylvia's closing of the office of Chancellor for Regional Campuses, an objective she had made clear as a candidate for the position, she became a Special Assistant to the President, Dean for Special Academic Programs (1975–76), and finally Special Assistant to the President for External Degree Programs (1976–1980) until her retirement.

She has published several books and innumerable articles on various areas of literature, as well as having given a number of lectures on literature, administration, correspondence, and futurism.

She founded and edited the Twayne Series: United States Authors (1959–76), English Authors (1962–75), World Authors (1964–76). During this editorship she assisted in the publication of over a thousand books, five hundred of which she edited personally.

Bowman holds memberships in the National Education Association, National Council of Teachers of English, American Association of University Professors, Modern Language Association (member of the Bibliography Committee), American Business Writers Association, American Association of University Women, Delta Kappa Gamma, Indiana English Council, International Platform Association, and the National Society of Literature and the Arts.

Sylvia was elected to Sigma Kappa Phi Delta (honorary) at Cantebury College and received a Boone County scholarship to Indiana University (1931). After entering academia, she continued to receive honors such as the Frederic Bachman Lieber Award for distinguished teaching (1962). The Centro

Studi Scambi Internazionali, an associate agency of UNESCO, presented her with the medal of honor and a diploma of the organization. The American Association of University Women named a scholarship in her honor (1967) and she was on their Scholarship Committee (1977–81). She was named "Woman of the Year" by Indianapolis Professional Chapter of Theta Sigma Phi (1972), and Indiana University Fort Wayne's senior class voted her their Distinguished Teaching Award (1969). Sylvia also was the recipient of the Professional Achievement Award of the University of Chicago Alumni Association (1973), an honorary LL.D. from St. Mary's College, Notre Dame, Indiana (1972), and The Helen Keller honorary D. Litt. from Urbana University, Urbana, Ohio (1981).

Ralph Edward Broyles, 1909–1975
CHANCELLOR, IU AT FORT WAYNE, 1969–1974

Ralph Edward Broyles, research chemist and administrator, son of William E. and Ellen (Evrard) Broyles, was born June 25, 1909, in Elwood, Indiana. The first eight years of Ralph's education took place in a one-room country school where one teacher taught all eight grades. The building was heated by two coal-burning stoves. He then attended Elwood High School (1927), and it was an instructor there who first instilled in him an interest in chemistry. All of Ralph's college work at Indiana University was in chemistry (A.B. 1932, M.A. 1933, Ph.D. 1942). At Indiana University Ralph participated in the ROTC program (1927–29). He was a member of the national honorary fraternities Sigma Xi and Phi Lambda Upsilon, as well as Alphi Chi Sigma fraternity.

Ralph married Catherine E. Williams, daughter of Dr. and Mrs. N. N. Williams of Mount Vernon, Indiana, on June 6, 1942.

After obtaining his M.A., Ralph worked as a research chemist for Aladdin Industries, Incorporated (1933–37). Broyles joined Indiana University as an assistant in the Chemistry Department while working on his Ph.D. (1937–41),

Ralph Edward Broyles

became an Extension Instructor in Chemistry (1941–46), and an Assistant Professor at the Fort Wayne Center (1950–51), and later became the Director (1951); Broyles was promoted to Associate Professor (1961) and Assistant Dean of University Extension (1962–66), and finally became Dean of the Fort Wayne campus (1966–69). The change in title from Director to Dean reflected the increased importance of regional campuses. When the school moved from an extension to a regional campus, Broyles was named Chancellor (1969–74). He held that position until retirement, when he was named Professor Emeritus and Chancellor Emeritus of Indiana University at Fort Wayne.

Broyles held membership in the American Chemical Society and was editor of *Retort,* its official publication (1945–46, 49–50). He belonged to Fort Wayne Chemists Club, Indiana Chemical Society, Indiana Academy of Science, American Association of University Professors, and Sigma Pi. He also had many civic connections, with memberships in the Chamber of Commerce, Fort Wayne Art School and Museum (and a member of its School Committee), Allen County United Chest Council (and chairman of its Salary and Personnel Committee), Education Committee of Senior Citizens, Incorporated of Fort Wayne and Allen County, and Lions. Ralph belonged to the First Presbyterian Church (and was a member of its Ruling Board of Elders) and was a Republican. He also found time to participate in many panels and discussion groups as well as to speak before various organizations in the area.

Broyles had many personal outside interests: he and his wife were avid fishermen; he liked to hunt, bowl and play bridge, was interested in handcrafts, and was a prolific reader. In the summertime he enjoyed gardening and had a veritable farm in his backyard.

Dr. Broyles died on June 24, 1975, while visiting his sister in Lynchburg, Virginia. His ashes are in the Columbarium of the First Presbyterian Church in Fort Wayne.

Edwin William Crooks

Edwin William Crooks, 1919–
CHANCELLOR, IU OF NEW ALBANY, 1969–

Edwin William Crooks, educator and administrator, son of Edwin William and Rebecca (Dils) Crooks, was born in Parkersburg, West Virginia, on July 29, 1919, where he attended school, graduating from Parkersburg High (1937). He then attended West Virginia University and obtained a B.S. in Business Administration (1941) and an M.A. (1942).

He was elected to Beta Gamma Sigma (business honorary), Phi Delta Kappa (education honorary), Scabbard and Blade (military honorary) and Phi Beta Kappa. He is a member of the Beta Theta Pi social fraternity (and also served as a faculty advisor) and, as a faculty member, was elected to the Phi Eta Sigma freshman honorary.

As a Lieutenant Commander in the U.S. Navy he saw active duty (1942–46) and continued in the Reserves until he retired (1966). After the war he continued his education at Harvard University, where he was awarded an M.B.A. (1947).

Crooks then accepted the position of Assistant to the President of The Halle Brothers Company in Cleveland, Ohio (1947–54). Meanwhile he married Joan Schleuniger on September 13, 1952, and they have three children: Edwin (born 1953), Ann (born 1955) and Alice (born 1958).

Returning to academia, Ed became Assistant Professor of Marketing (1954–56) at West Virginia University. He then moved to Bloomington and attended Indiana University to obtain a D.B.A. (1959), while holding a Ford Foundation Fellowship (1956–58). Returning to teaching at West Virginia University (1958–66), he held the position of Professor of Marketing and Assistant Dean in the School of Business.

The sudden death of Dr. Byron F. Laird, Director of Indiana University's Southeast Campus, left a void which Edwin Crooks was called upon to fill (1966), at first with the title of Dean, later changed to Acting Chancellor (1968). He continued to hold an academic appointment as Professor of Business Administration during his years of service at IUS and regularly taught courses in marketing. In September 1969, Crooks became the Chancellor of Indiana University Southeast.

Under his leadership the Southeast campus grew from 2408 students, 69 full-time faculty and professional staff, and 37 classified staff in 1970 to 4336 students, 124 full-time faculty and professional staff, and 89 classified staff in 1980. Available academic programs tripled during this decade, and extracurricular activities likewise grew, encouraged by available facilities in the University Center and Activities Building. The Southeast campus moved from downtown Jeffersonville in May 1973 to a new campus at the northern edge of New Albany. There was twice the space at the new campus, and four buildings have since been added in 1975, '76 and '79.

Crooks is the author of several monographs on retailing practices. He has held memberships in the American Marketing and Southern Marketing Associations, Retired Officers Association, and the Board of Directors of the Dils Brothers and Company Department Store.

Civic service has not been overlooked by Ed, and he has served on numerous Boards of Directors: Rotary Club (also past President), Southern Indiana Symphony Orchestra (1966–68), Steamboat Museum (1969–71), Community Action Agency (also Treasurer, 1974–79), Clark County Chamber of Commerce (1971–74, 79–82), New Albany Chamber of Commerce (1974–77), Clark County United Way (1967–72), Leadership Louisville (1979–81), and Kentuckiana Metroversity (1969–81, also past President). He is a past Council Vice-President and member of the executive board of the Boy Scouts, member of the Economic Development Council (1973–75), member Friends of the Library (President, 1978–80), and member of Metro United Way (Education Division Chairman, 1981). He attends the Wall Street United Methodist Church.

Joseph Paul Giusti 1935–
Chancellor, IU at Fort Wayne, 1979–

Joseph Paul Giusti, educator and administrator, son of Joseph and Elena (Carletti) Giusti, was born on March 4, 1935, in Harrisburg, Pennsylvania, where he attended grammar and

Joseph Paul Guisti

high schools. Joe obtained a B.A. at Villanova University (1957) and went on to Pennsylvania State University for his graduate work (M.A. 1959, D. Ed. 1962). At Pennsylvania State, Joe was elected to the national honorary fraternity, Pi Gamma Mu, and was a member of Phi Delta Kappa and Alpha Kappa Psi.

Joe married Marie D. Mazza of Harrisburg, Pennsylvania, on January 30, 1960, and they had three daughters: Jeannine Carolyn, Lynn Christine, and Susan Marie.

Giusti became Assistant to the Vice-President for Academic Affairs at Pennsylvania State (1963–65), after receiving his doctorate there. He also had the title of Assistant Professor of Education (1964–1969). He became Director of the Beaver Campus (1965–June, 1979) and an Associate Member of the Graduate Faculty (1965–68); and later, he was Associate Professor of Higher Education (1969–June, 1979).

Joe has been the recipient of the Benjamin Rush Award from the Medical Society of Beaver County, Pennsylvania (1976), and the Distinguished Service Award from the Beaver Campus Advisory Board (1974). Since leaving Beaver Campus, the Pennsylvania State Board of Trustees further honored Giusti by naming the outdoor amphitheater of the Beaver Campus-Community Center for him and by establishing the J. P. Guisti Literary Collection at the Beaver Campus Library.

While he was living in Pennsylvania, Joe was active in civic affairs as well as those of the campus. He was a member of the Advisory Committee of the Vocational Education Management Information System of the Commonwealth of Pennsylvania (1971–79). He served on the Board of Directors of the Medical Center of Beaver County (1972–79, President, 1972–75; Director Emeritus, 1975); was Chairman of the Beaver County Council of Higher Learning (1974–79); a member of the Board of Delegates, Christian Associates of Southwest Pennsylvania (1970–73); and a member of the Board of Directors, Beaver County Mental Health Society (1969–74).

In 1976 he was awarded an honorary D. Litt. by St. Vincent College, and in 1982 he was made an honorary lifetime member of the IUPU/FW Alumni Association.

Since coming to Fort Wayne, Giusti has become involved with such community affairs as the Parkview Hospital (Board) of Directors), Greater Fort Wayne Chamber of Commerce (Board of Directors), Joint Advisory Council of the Fort Wayne Medical Education Program, Fort Wayne Public Television, Inc. (Board of Directors), Fort Wayne Future, Inc. (Executive Committee), and the Fort Wayne Educational Foundation. He attends the Cathedral of the Immaculate Conception Church.

Glenn Allan Goerke, 1931–

CHANCELLOR, IU AT RICHMOND, 1981–

Glenn Allan Goerke, educator and administrator, son of Albert W. and Cecil P. (Crowl) Goerke, was born in Lincoln Park, Michigan, on May 15, 1931. He attended local schools through high school and then matriculated at Eastern Michigan University, where he was awarded an A.B. (1952) and an M.A. (1955). He moved on to Michigan State University for his Ph.D. (1964). Glenn was a member of Phi Delta Kappa education fraternity and Arm of Honor at East Michigan University.

After obtaining his A.B., Goerke worked with several secondary school systems in Michigan as a teacher of mentally and emotionally disturbed students and as a principal at both an elementary and a secondary school (1952–63). In late 1963 he moved to Florida and became the administrator at a residential State Center, as well as the coordinator of a Civil Defense Extension Program at Florida Institute for Continuing Studies (1963–64), advancing to Dean of the Division of General Extension (1964–66).

Moving over to the Florida Board of Regents, Glenn became Coordinator of Non-Credit Activities (1965–66), Director of its Office of Continuing Education (1966–68), and Director of Academic Program Planning and Coordination (1968–70).

In April 1970, Goerke accepted the positions of Dean in the Division of University Services and Continuing Education and Professor of Education at Florida International University

Glenn Allan Goerke

(1970-71). He moved to the position of Associate Dean and Acting Provost of the Interama Campus (1971-72); Associate Vice-President for Academic Affairs, Dean of Faculties and Acting Provost of the North Miami Campus (1972-73); Vice-President for Community Affairs (1973-77); and then relinquished all administrative positions to return to full-time teaching as Professor of Adult Education on the Miami Campus (1977-78).

Goerke finally left the International University for the position of Dean of the Division of University Extension and Summer Session at the University of Rhode Island (1978-81). He became Chancellor of IU East on April 1, 1981.

Glenn married Joyce Leslie Walker on March 3, 1973. Glenn had three children by a previous marriage: Lynne E. (born 1958), Jill A. (born 1961), and Kurt E. (born 1962).

Glenn has published numerous articles in professional journals and has written monographs for the Florida Board of Regents.

He is a member of the National University Continuing Education Association, having served in numerous capacities (Board of Directors, 1970-75, Secretary, 1971-72; President-Elect, 1972-73; President, 1973-74); Southeast Region Dean and Directors Executive Board (1968- ; Vice-Chairman, 1968-69; Chairman 1969-70); Adult Education Association, USA (Florida State Delegate, 1966-70); Commission on Research (1967-68); NASULGC Chairman, Council on Extension Committee on Relationships with Other Institutions (1970-71); Executive Board, Council on Extension (1967-71, 1978-81); Committee on Intra-University Relationships (1967-68); Committee on Business and Technology (1966-67); and Delegate to Urban Affairs Committee 1980. Goerke has also filled the role of consultant in program development for the governments of the Bahamas, Jamaica, El Salvador, and Columbia (1975-77). He also administered the first VISTA training program in the United States and initiated statewide labor and women's institutions in Florida.

Civic involvement also has been a part of Glenn's busy life in the various locales in which he has been employed. He was a board member of the International Center, Inc., in Miami

(1973-75); Chairman of Kiwanis Committee on Physically Handicapped Youth (1976-77); a member of the Miami-Bogota Sister Cities Alliance (Vice President, 1975; President 1976-77); Miami Committee for Visiting Dignitaries (1977); United Fund (Vice-Chairman for the University of Rhode Island, 1979); AFL/CIO Advisory Committee, Institute for Labor Studies and Research (1978); several United Way Committees (1974-75); and the Florida Governor's Planning Council on Criminal Justice, Region III.

He is a member of Richmond Symphony Orchestra Board of Directors, Richmond Area Chamber of Commerce (Board of Directors; Vice-President, 1982), and the Indiana Arts Commission Advisory Panel on Education.

Frederick Andrew Grohsmeyer, Jr., 1923–
Director at Richmond, 1973–1976

Frederick Andrew Grohsmeyer, Jr., psychologist and industrial consultant, son of Frederick Andrew and Margaret Emma (Kerl) Grohsmeyer, was born April 7, 1923, in Canton, Ohio, where he attended secondary school. His college work was taken at four different schools. He obtained a Certificate in Pre-Meteorology from Hamilton College in Clinton, New York (1944); A.B. from DePauw (1948); M.A. from Northwestern University (1949); and Ph.D. from Purdue (1954).

Frederick married Sarah Alice Dudley of Elwood, Indiana, on June 19, 1949, and they had two children: Margaret Anne (Mrs. Michael Judson), and Erik Andrew.

Frederick was in the U.S. Air Force (1943-1946). After obtaining his M.A., he joined the faculty of Earlham College (1949) as an Assistant Professor of Psychology and also became a member of the Earlham Institute for Executive Growth (1951). He then spent two-and-a-half years in the field of Industrial Counseling with Rohrer, Hibler, and Replogle in Minneapolis (1956-57), and with Booz, Allen, and Hamilton in Chicago (1957-58), returning to Earlham as Director of the Institute for Executive Growth and Associate Professor of Psychology (1958-64). Grohsmeyer continued as Consultant

Frederick Andrew Grohsmeyer, Jr.

and Lecturer for the Institute (1964–73), meanwhile he served as Chairman of the Division of Social Science (1967), Chairman of the Psychology Department (1964–67), and Professor of Psychology and Dean of the General Studies Division (1969–71).

In 1971 Grohsmeyer became Director of the IU East Campus and Professor of Psychology, guiding the campus through its early growth and the construction of its first building (1974). This campus has been one of the fastest growing in the IU system and has developed numerous cooperative programs with other Indiana Schools to meet the needs of the area. Grohsmeyer resigned as of January 1, 1976, to return to fulltime teaching at IU East.

Frederick holds professional memberships in the American Psychological Association, Indiana Psychological Association, American Arbitration Society, Federal Mediation and Conciliation Service, Society of Professionals in Dispute Resolution, AAAS, and Sigma Xi. He has contributed a number of professional articles to *Choice* and *Labor Arbitration Awards* and is a popular lecturer. Since 1975 he has been a Lecturer in the U.S. Army's Professional Military Education program.

He is a member of the Wayne County MS Association (Chairman of the 1962 Fund Drive); Rotary (President of Richmond Chapter, 1979–80); We Americans, Inc., (President 1975–77); East Indiana Community College, Inc., (Treasurer, 1970–80); First Presbyterian Church (elder 1968–); and has held board memberships for the Central Methodist Church, Mental Health Association, Yokefellow Institute, Richmond Industrial Ministry, Richmond Symphony, and the First-Presbyterian Church. He also has served as Chairman of the Citizens Committee to Investigate Racial/Police Conflict and Propose Corrective Action (appointed by the Mayor), consultant to Richmond Police and Fire Departments, and Chairman of the Committee to Develop a Police Merit System. He is a member of the Board of Directors of the Peoples Home and Savings Association and of the Richmond Block Company (Chairman of the Board).

He was the recipient of the second annual Outstanding Faculty Award given by the IU East Alumni (1978).

Maynard Kiplinger Hine, 1907–
CHANCELLOR, IUPUI, 1968–1973

Maynard Kiplinger Hine, dentist, educator and administrator, son of Clyde L. and Delia (Kiplinger) Hine, was born in Waterloo, Indiana, on August 25, 1907. He graduated from Illinois Community High School in Tuscola (1925). Maynard went on to college at the University of Illinois, where he obtained his D.D.S. (1930) and an M.S. in Dental Pathology and Therapeutics (1932).

In the year he obtained his M.S., he also married Harriet Foulke on April 30, 1932 (deceased 1972), and they had three children: Maynard Kiplinger, Jr. (B.S. Oberlin College 1954), now a physicist in Washington, DC; Judith (Mrs. John Hyde, B.S. 1959, M.S. 1973) who now resides in Bethesda, Maryland, and William Clyde (Ed.D. 1973), Assistant Dean, University of Evansville.

After two years in private practice with his father in Tuscola, Illinois (1932–34), Hine had the opportunity to do research at the University of Rochester (1934–36) with a Rockefeller Fellowship (1934–35) and a Carnegie Fellowship (1935–36). He then returned to the University of Illinois' Department of Oral Pathology and Periodontics (1936–44), and in 1944 was appointed Professor and Head of the Department of Oral Histopathology and Periodontics at Indiana University; a year later he became the Dean (1945). He was the Chancellor of Indiana University at Indianapolis from November 1, 1968 to 1973. When Purdue University's Indianapolis Campus merged with that of Indiana University (1969), he continued as Chancellor of IUPUI until his retirement from administration (September, 1973), at which time he became a Special Consultant to the University President, an Executive Associate of the IU Foundation, and Professor of Periodontics.

Hine has been a prolific writer, having co-authored five books and contributed numerous articles to a variety of scientific journals, as well as editing the *Journal of Periodontology* (1950–1970). He has received most of the honors awarded by various local and national organizations allied to the field of dentistry. He is a past President of the American Association

Maynard Kiplinger Hine

of Dental Schools (1953); International Association for Dental Research (1952); American Association of Dental Editors (1948); American Association of Endodontists (1947); Indianapolis District Dental Society (1952); American Fund for Dental Health (1958-62); Indiana State Dental Association (1957-58), receiving its Distinguished Service Award (1974); American Academy of Periodontology (1964), which presented him with its annual gold medal (1969); Indianapolis Center for Advanced Research (1970-75); the international dental organization, Federation Dentaire Internationale (1975-77); the American Dental Association (1965-66), receiving its Distinguished Service Award (1975); and the American Academy of the History of Dentistry (1980-81). In addition he has been honored with the honorary degree of Doctor of Science by various universities, as follows: Case Western Reserve University (1967), University of Illinois (1969), Boston University (1970), Ohio State University (1970), Temple University (1973), Marian College, Indianapolis (1973), and Indiana University (1979). He has received innumerable awards from a wide variety of organizations. He also has been awarded memberships in the American Academy of Dental Science, Boston; American Association of Endodontists (1969); American Academy of Maxillofacial Prosthetics (1969); American Academic of Periodontology; American Dental Society of Iceland (1974); and the Indiana American Revolution Bicentennial Commission (1974).

Hine is a Founder Diplomate of the American Board of Endodontics; member of the Council on Dentistry of the V.A. Medical Case Program; Consultant to U.S. Air Force School of Aviation Medicine (1952-53); Fellow of American Academy of Oral Pathology; Fellow of the American College of Dentists; Fellow of the International College of Dentists (Vice-Regent, District Seven, 1967; degree of Master 1981); Fellow of the Royal College of Surgeons of Ireland (1974), of the Philippines (1977), of Canada (1977); Councillor of the Federation Dentaire Internationale (and member and advisor of its Commission on Classification and Statistics for Oral Conditions; and an advisor to the Commission on Dental Practice, all for the years 1968 to 70; President, 1975-77); and he served on Indiana State Board of Health (1947–; Chairman, 1959–61).

Dr. Hine also holds memberships in Sigma Xi (Treasurer of College of Medicine Chapter, 1942–44); Omicron Kappa Upsilon, dental honorary, (Executive Council, Sigma Chapter, 1940–41; Secretary-Treasurer, 1941–42; Vice-President, 1942–43; President, 1943–44); Delta Sigma Delta, receiving its award for Meritorious Service (1968); Phi Eta Sigma; Literary, Torch, Columbia and Indianapolis Athletic Clubs. He is a Rotarian, a Republican, and an elder in the Presbyterian Church. He has been on many civic boards, including the Central Indiana Council on Aging, (President, 1980–82), Board of Channel 20 TV, Board of Indiana Health Careers, Board of Indiana Science Foundation, and has served on innumerable committees.

Special honors bestowed on Dr. Hine include two "Sagamore of the Wabash," Kentucky Colonel, Tennessee Traveler, Indiana Tribe Chief (Oklahoma), "Honorary Inmate" of Kansas State Penitentiary (1981), Member Board of Trustees of Jack Daniels University, and an Honorary Membership in the American Association of Dental Insultants (a national fun group of professionals, limited to one hundred members, started when "consultants" became such a craze).

With all of his professional and civic involvement, he still has found time to pursue his interests in artifacts of American Indians left in the area, philately, and the collection of old maps of Indiana. He also continues to be active in numerous university affairs as well as civic and educational organizations.

Robert Joseph McNeill, 1921–
Chancellor, IU at Gary, 1970–1974

Robert Joseph McNeill, political scientist and public administrator, son of Joseph and Mae (Moody) McNeill, was born in Minneapolis, Minnesota, on November 2, 1921. He attended local schools through high school and then matriculated at the University of Minnesota, where he received his B.A. (1943). He later took an M.A. (1953) and a Ph.D. (1959) at the University of California/Berkeley.

Robert Joseph McNeill

Robert married Evelyn Regina Young on December 28, 1949.

McNeill was employed as an accountant in private industry (1943-45) and then served as a civilian accountant/budget officer with the Army in Tokyo (1946-50). Upon his return to the United States in 1950, he enrolled at the University of California at Berkeley, where he also served as area consultant for the International Institute of Education (1951-54), was a Public Administration Analyst (1951-54), a teaching assistant (1954-56), and then an Assistant Professor of Government at Los Angeles State College (1956-57). He moved to Purdue University (1957-64) as Assistant Professor of Government, during which period he was also Special Assistant to the Governor on a National Center for Education in Politics fellowship (1962-63). With an extension of the fellowship (1963-64), he worked on the Democratic National Committee.

In 1964, McNeill accepted the Directorship of the Government Management Program at Wayne State University, where he also held the rank of Associate Professor of Political Science (1964-67). Accepting the management of the Graduate Administration Program at Pennsylvania State University, Robert moved to its Capital Campus with the rank of Professor of Administration (1967-69), broadened his responsibilities to include that of Business Regional Planning as well as Administration, and became Chairman of the Capital Campus Research Council (1969-70). He then accepted the chancellorship of Indiana University at Gary, where he remained until he resigned for health reasons in July 1974. He took a semester's administrative leave and returned to teaching in January 1975, but found he had to request additional sick leave and finally resigned in August 1975.

While Chancellor, Robert McNeill was active in civic affairs, serving the Teamsters, Anderson Company, and Inland-Ryerson Scholarship Committees, Lake County Coordinating Council of the Indiana Criminal Justice Agency, Community Advisory Council of the Northwest Center for Medical Education, IUPU/Calumet Region Board of Advisors, Advisory Committee of the Lake County Community Development Commission, Board of Directors of the Gary Chamber of

Commerce (also its Education Committee), East Chicago Chamber of Commerce, and Hammond Chamber of Commerce.

McNeill held memberships in ASPA, American Political Science Association, ISPA (Executive Committee); American Association for Higher Education Conference; American Council for Education; Academy of Political Science; Midwest Conference of Political Scientists, Northeast Political Science Association; AAUP; Pi Sigma Alpha; Merrillville Rotary; Indiana Society of Chicago; and the University Club.

He was the co-editor of a book with Stanley E. Seashore, the author of numerous articles and monographs, as well as a reviewer of books in his field of expertise. During his chancellorship he made numerous public appearances and speeches on behalf of the University.

Danilo Orescanin, 1932–
Chancellor, IU at Gary, 1975–

Danilo Orescanin, administrator and educator, son of George and Nellie (Kukich) Orescanin, was born April 7, 1932, in Mingo Junction, Ohio, where he went to secondary school. He obtained a B.S. (1953) at West Virginia University and then spent a year in the U.S. Army as a Corporal in Military Police (1954–55). He continued his education at Indiana University, obtaining an M.B.A. (1954) and a D.B.A. (1960).

Meanwhile, he married Kathleen Virginia Wolfe of Rowlesburg, West Virginia, on June 19, 1954, and they had two children: Danilo II (A.B. Political Science 1978) and Lori (B.S. in Business 1981).

While Dan worked on his M.B.A. and D.B.A., he was a Graduate Assistant in the School of Business (1953–54), a Teaching Associate in Management (1957–58), and Lecturer in Business Administration (1958–60), adding the responsibility of Administrative Assistant to the Dean (1959–60). He resigned in August 1960 to become Assistant Professor of Business and Assistant Coordintor of Evening and Summer Schools at the University of South Florida in Tampa (1960–

Danilo Orescanin

63). Orescanin returned to Indiana University as Assistant Professor of Business Administration and Assistant Dean, Division of University Extension (January 1963–June 1965) and then returned to full-time teaching (July 1965–June 1968).

Indiana University sent Dan to be the Resident Advisor of its program at the University of Dacca, East Pakistan (August 1965–July 1967). When he returned from Pakistan he became Assistant Dean of Research and Advanced Studies (September 1967–June 1968), moving up to Associate Dean (July 1968–June 1969). Dan added the task of Assistant to the President to his Associate Dean duties (July 1969–January 1972) and then resigned in January 1972 to become the Executive Assistant to the President of Southern Illinois University. In July 1972 he became Vice-President for Administration and Campus Treasurer, and was named Executive Vice-President in July 1973. He stepped down from the latter position (March 1974), but continued to teach as Professor of Business Administration until September 1975, at which time he was called back to Indiana University to become Chancellor of Indiana University at Gary (September 1975), where he also holds the rank of Professor of Business Administration.

He received the merit award of the Society for the Advancement of Management (1972–75), the second such award ever made. Orescanin holds memberships in the American Economics Association, Academy of Management, the honorary fraternity of Tau Kappa Epislon, Alpha Kappa Psi, Beta Gamma Sigma, Sigma Iota Epsilon, and Phi Delta Kappa. Dan received the first award for outstanding contributions and service from the Association of Teacher Educators that was ever given to a non-education faculty member (1979). He also received the Outstanding Citizen's Award from the Indiana University Dons (1979).

He has authored a number of research articles published in business journals, and he was a contributor to the book, *Critical Incidents in Management* by Champion and Bridges.

Both in Illinois and Indiana, Dan has been very involved with civic affairs. He speaks frequently to various community organizations and serves on a variety of boards and committees such as the Chamber of Commerce (President, Gary,

1977-79); Community Development; Scholarship Committees; Mental Health Association (Lake County: Second Vice-President, 1978-79; First Vice-President, 1979-80; President, 1980-81); United Way (Vice-Chairman, 1976-77; Vice-Chairman of Lake Area, 1979; Board of Directors, 1978-; Chairman, 1981-82); First Congressional District Educator's Advisory Committee (1977-); American Red Cross (Board of Directors, 1976-); Editorial Advisory Board of the *Post Tribune* (1978-); Presidential White House Fellowship Committee (Select Panel, 1978, 1979); Magistrate Nominating Committee for Northern District of Indiana (1981-); and many more.

Orescanin also has served as a member of a number of international groups. He was the U.S. Delegate to the International Seminar on "The University Today" sponsored by the League of Yugoslavians (July 1964), a seminar participant (August 1979); member of the Venezuelan Survey Team (MUSCIA, 1968-70); and a member of the Advisory Committee for AID Programs with East Pakistan Agricultural University at Mymensingh (MUSCIA, 1970).

Kenneth Earl Penrod, 1916–
Provost, IU Medical Center, 1965-1969

Kenneth Earl Penrod, physiologist and educator, son of William F. and Josie Alma (Carman) Penrod, was born March 30, 1916, in Blanchester, Ohio. He graduated from the Troy, Ohio, high school (1934) and then attended Miami University, where he obtained a B.S. (1938). He became a member of Phi Kappa Tau social fraternity, was elected to Phi Beta Kappa and to Alpha Omega Alpha medical honorary. Ken did his graduate work at Iowa State (Ph.D. 1942) and then became an aviation physiologist for the United States Air Force (1942-46), reaching the rank of Captain. He worked at the Aeromedical Research Laboratory in Ohio and served in the North Pacific and European Theatres. He is the co-holder of a patent on the design of a spacesuit helmet.

Ken married Virginia B. Hogue of Kansas City, Missouri, on June 29, 1942 and they had two children: Caroline (born 1947) and Bruce (born 1949).

Kenneth Earl Penrod

Upon discharge from the Air Force, Penrod entered academia as Assistant Professor of Physiology at Boston University's School of Medicine (1946–50). He then joined the faculty of Duke University's School of Medicine as Associate Professor of Physiology (1950–57), was promoted to full Professor (1957–59), and became Assistant Dean of the School of Medicine (1952–59). Ken was named by West Virginia University as Vice-President for Medical Affairs, a position newly created in connection with West Virginia's new Medical Center (1959–65). The position of Provost of the Indiana University Medical Center in Indianapolis was created by the Board of Trustees in 1965 at the behest of President Stahr, who believed it would improve the administrative organization of the Medical Center. Stahr had been President of West Virginia University when he brought Penrod there from Duke University, and Stahr now brought him to Indiana.

Penrod was a prolific writer and researcher as well as a widely known medical administrator. He is the author of innumerable professional articles. He holds memberships in a number of professional organizations such as AAAS, American Physiological Society, Association for Academic Health Centers, Association of American Medical Colleges, Sigma Xi, and the Rotary Club. He was a member of the editorial board of the *Journal of Medical Education* (1957–65) and the *Journal of Experimental Sciences* (1960–70).

Penrod resigned in 1969 and accepted an appointment as the Vice-Chancellor for Medical and Health Sciences at the State University System of Florida, a position entailing the planning and coordination of the developing programs in the health sciences at Florida's seven existing and two planned public university campuses (1969–74). He became Director of the Community Hospital Graduate Medical Education Program for the Florida Board of Regents at Tallahassee in 1974.

Alexander F. Schilt, 1941–
CHANCELLOR, IU AT RICHMOND, 1976–1980

Alexander F. Schilt, educator and administrator, son of Louis F. and Alice (Hinton) Schilt, was born on March 4, 1941, in Cheyenne, Wyoming, where he went to secondary school, graduating from Laramie High School (1959). He studied for his B.A. at the University of Wyoming (1964) and then moved to Arizona State University for his graduate work (M.A. 1966, Ph.D. 1969). While a student at Arizona, Alex held several positions: Head Resident (1964–65), Assistant Dean and Complex Director (1965–69), and Assistant Director for Financial Aids (1969–70).

Alex married Charlotte Snyder of Phoenix, Arizona, on May 27, 1967, and they had two children: Paige Eileen (born 1971) and Kristen Rose (born 1974).

Schilt came to Indiana University as Dean of Student Services and Assistant Professor of Education (1970–75) at Indiana University Southeast. In 1975 his academic rank was raised to Associate Professor with tenure. In March 1976 he moved to Indiana University East at Richmond as Dean of that campus and Professor of Education (March 1976–1978). With the development and expansion of IU East, Schilt's title was changed to Chancellor (September, 1978).

The extensive contacts developed by Schilt in Richmond and his civic involvement there supported and increased the close ties between the citizens of Richmond and Indiana University East. He was active in the Chamber of Commerce, serving on the Richmond Board of Directors, as Vice-President for Government Relations, and on the Education Committee and the Downtown Committee; he was on the Board of Directors of the Whitewater Opera Company, the Rotary, and Leadership Wayne County, Inc.; and served as a member of the Indiana Council for Economic Education.

Alex holds membership in a number of professional organizations related to his academic specialty, as well as other organizations: American Association of Personnel and Guidance, American Association of Teacher Education, American Association for Higher Education, American Association of

Alexander F. Schilt

University Professors, American College Personnel Association, American Educational Research Association, American Association of State Colleges and Universities, Indiana Society of Chicago, and Kappa Delta Pi education honorary. He attends the Catholic Church.

Schilt resigned as Chancellor in 1980 to assume the chancellorship of the downtown campus of the University of Houston, where he also holds the rank of Professor of Psychology.

Donald Schwartz, 1927–
Chancellor, IUPU at Fort Wayne, 1974–1978

Donald Schwartz, chemist and administrator, son of Harry A. and Ethel (Rabinowitz) Schwartz, was born on December 27, 1927, in Scarsdale, New York, and attended local schools through high school. He obtained his B.S. at the University of Missouri (1949) and then attended Montana State University for an M.S. (1951). Don obtained a Ph.D. at Pennsylvania State University (1955) and did postdoctoral work at the University of California at Berkeley (1958).

Don married Lois Schwartz of Bridgeport, Connecticut, on September 8, 1948, and they had four children: Leanne (Mrs. Brilliant), Mark W., Scott B., and Bradley F.

In 1955 Schwartz became Assistant Professor of Chemistry at Villanova University. After his postdoctoral work in California, he moved to Moorhead State College, Minnesota, as an Assistant Professor of Chemistry (1958–59), then to North Dakota State University as Professor of Chemistry (1959–66). He was Program Director at the National Science Foundation (1966–69), and in 1969–70 he became Associate Dean of the Graduate School and Director of Research at Memphis State University. He moved again the next year to become Dean for Advanced Studies with the rank of full Professor at Florida Atlantic University in Boca Ratan (1970–71).

Don accepted the position of Vice-President for Academic Affairs (1971) at SUNY/Buffalo and became its Acting President in 1974. He held this position until he accepted the chancellorship at Indiana/Purdue University in Fort Wayne

Donald Schwartz

(1974–March 1978), which he resigned to become the Chancellor of the University of Colorado at Colorado Springs (1978–).

Schwartz holds memberships in the American Chemical Society, AAAS, Sigma XI, Phi Lambda Upsilon, Phi Delta Kappa, Downtown Rotary of Colorado Springs, Colorado Springs Chamber of Commerce, Masonic Order, and the Shrine.

Schwartz continued to maintain his interest in research while he held administrative positions. He is a prolific author and has published innumerable articles in scientific journals, mainly in chemistry.

Hugh Lee Thompson, 1934–
CHANCELLOR, IU AT KOKOMO, 1980–

Hugh Lee Thompson, educator and administrator, son of Frank Leslie and Althea Electa (Brown) Thompson, was born in Martinsburg, West Virginia, on March 25, 1934. He graduated from Martinsburg High School (1952) and was granted a B.A. from Shepherd College (Shepherdstown, West Virginia, 1956). While studying at the latter school, Hugh was a member of the football, basketball, and swimming teams. He moved to Pennsylvania State University for an M.A. (1958) and to Case Western Reserve University for his Ph.D. (1969). He worked as a Graduate Assistant at Pennsylvania State (1956–57) and as an Instructor at Pennsylvania State (1957–60), Akron University (1960–62), and Baldwin-Wallace (1962–66).

Hugh became Assistant to the President, and Assistant Professor of Education at Baldwin-Wallace College (1966–69) and later became Director of Institutional Planning, continuing as an Assistant to the President (1969–70). He took a leave of absence for a year to become the Coordinator for Associated Colleges of Cleveland (1970–71). Upon completion of the Cleveland project, Thompson assumed the presidency of Siena Heights College (Michigan, 1971–77) and eventually

Hugh Lee Thompson

moved to the presidency of Detroit Institute of Technology (1977–80).

Hugh married Patricia Smith of Hagerstown, Maryland, on October 16, 1952, and they had four children: Cheri (born 1953), Linda (born 1954), Tempe (born 1960), and Vicki (born 1962).

Thompson has given innumerable speeches before civic groups, has made many TV appearances, and has attended a number of institutes in connection with his various past positions. He also has published numerous articles in professional journals.

Thompson has been very active in civic, philanthropic, and religious organizations at each of his home locations. He has served on the Boards of Directors of such organizations as the Goodwill Industries, Chamber of Commerce, Lutheran Church, Finance Board of Lenawee County, YMCA, Detroit Public School's Advisory Board on Career Counseling and Placement, and Advisory Action Council of the Adrian Training School. He has worked with the PTA, Cleveland Catholic Charities, and has aided Berea officials in preparing Federal proposals.

Since moving to Kokomo, Thompson has become a member of the Boards of Directors of the Creative Arts Council, Kokomo-Howard County Chamber of Commerce, American Cancer Society (Chairman, Public Education Committee), United Way (Chairman, Pilot Campaign for 1981), Kokomo Civic Theatre, and the Kokomo Symphonic Society. He is a member of the Rotary Club, Cross Lutheran Church, Kokomo Development Corporation Board, and the Christian Business Men's Committee.

Hugh's professional memberships include the American Association for Higher Education, American Association of University Administrators, American Management Association, National Urban Education Association, Association of Institutional Research, Society for College and University Planning, National Association of College Admissions Counselors, Phi Delta Kappa, Kappa Delta Pi, American Association of Presidents of Independent Colleges and Universities, Economic Club, Capital Hill Club, Michigan Academy of Science, Arts and Letters, and the Engineering Society of Detroit.

His social affiliations include the Columbia Club (Indianapolis), Elks Club, Kokomo Country Bluc, Masons, Scottish Rite, Shriners, Worldwide Sportsmen's Club, Detroit Athletic Club, and the Detroit Club.

Lester Marvin Wolfson, 1923–
Chancellor, IU at South Bend, 1969–

Lester Marvin Wolfson, educator and administrator, son of William and Bess (Silverman) Wolfson, was born in Evansville on September 13, 1923. His family later moved to Michigan, and he graduated from Union High School in Grand Rapids (1941). He was freshman class president, was active in dramatics, debate, and choral music, and edited the school paper. Wolfson received local and state speech awards, a national essay award, and the Kech prize for creative writing. Covaledictorian of his graduating class, he won the Dillingham Memorial Cup for scholarship and leadership.

Wolfson went on to the University of Michigan, where he obtained both his undergraduate (A.B. 1945), and graduate degrees (M.A. 1946; Ph.D. 1954). At college he continued to receive honors for his work. He was elected to Phi Eta Sigma (1942), Phi Beta Kappa (1944), and Phi Kappa Phi (1945). He received a Hopwood Essay Award (1942), was a Hunt Scholar (1943–44), a Student Aid Foundation Scholar (1944–45), an Association of American Colleges (1945–46), University Fellow (1947–48), and a Rockham Predoctoral Fellow (1948–50).

At college Wolfson met and married Esther Evans of Grand Rapids, Michigan, on July 3, 1949. (Esther later obtained an M.S. from IU at South Bend, 1974.) They have three children, all of whom attend IU: Alice Jeannette (expects to obtain a degree in May 1983), Margaret Gail (A.B. 1975), and George Stephen.

At the University of Michigan, while Wolfson was engaged in graduate studies, he was employed as a Teaching Fellow in English (1945–47). He also taught English at Wayne Univer-

Lester Marvin Wolfson

sity (1950–53) and at the University of Houston (Assistant Professor, English and Speech, 1953–55). He came to Indiana University's Northwest Campus as Assistant Professor of English (1955–61). During 1958–59 school year, Wolfson took a leave of absence to teach as visiting Assistant Professor of English at the University of California at Santa Barbara. In addition to his duties as Assistant Professor of English at Indiana University, he assumed the duties of Academic Counselor (1960–63), was promoted to Associate Professor (1961), became Assistant Chairman of the Department of English at the Northwest Campus (February 1964–June 1964), moved to the South Bend Campus as Director and Assistant Dean of the Division of University Extension (July 1964–April 1966); and was promoted to Professor of English (1967). With the continued growth of the University, he was made Dean of the South Bend/Mishawaka Campus (1966–69) and finally, with the reorganization of the University into regional campuses, he became Acting Chancellor at South Bend (1968) and Chancellor (1969).

Wolfson is the author of several articles and reviews which have been published in professional journals. He holds memberships in a number of organizations related to his discipline such as the Modern Language Association, the College English Association, the National Council of Teachers of English, and the American Association of University Professors. Even with his heavy load of teaching and administrative duties, Wolfson still has found time to serve the community. He sits on the Boards of Directors of several area organizations, including the South Bend Symphony Orchestra Association, the Michiana Arts and Sciences Council (President 1974–75), the Michiana Public Broadcasting Corporation, the Stanley Clark School, the Civic Center Foundation, and the Memorial Hospital of South Bend.

Secretaries and Treasurers

Thomas Aubrey Cookson

Thomas Aubrey Cookson, 1881–1969
ASSISTANT SECRETARY, February 11, 1936—June 12, 1936
SECRETARY, 1936–1937
TREASURER, 1937–1942
SECRETARY, 1942–1951

Thomas Aubrey Cookson, of Monroe County, who became Registrar of Indiana University and Secretary to the Board of Trustees, was born at Cleveland, Ohio, January 5, 1881, the son of George and Eliza Jane Cookson. In Cleveland he attended the grade schools. In 1892 his parents moved to Anderson, Indiana, where Thomas continued school work and was graduated from Anderson High School in June, 1900.

In September, 1902, he entered Indiana University where he was in attendance intermittently until 1907. In 1907–1908 Mr. Cookson was assistant cashier of the Citizens Loan and Trust Company, of Bloomington. He was Assistant to the Bursar, and then Assistant Bursar, 1908–1920. He was on leave of absence during the School Year 1919–1920. Appointed Assistant Registrar in 1920, he continued to serve in that capacity until June 12, 1936. Then, on the retirement of Mr. Cravens, he was appointed Registrar, in which capacity he continued to serve until 1948.

On February 11, 1936, Mr. Cookson also was appointed Assistant Secretary of the Board of Trustees, succeeding Mr. Cravens. On June 12, 1936, he was made Secretary, and served until July 1, 1937, when he became Treasurer of the University, and Ward G. Biddle became Secretary to the Board. Mr. Cookson was Treasurer and Mr. Biddle Secretary for five years (1937–1942). On August 1, 1942, Mr. Cookson again became Secretary to the Board and served until 1951 when he retired.

Tommy married Mignon White (A.B. 1911) on October 20, 1915, and they had three children: Ruth Eliza (B.S. 1944; deceased November 21, 1980), Clara Louise (Mrs. J. Hugh Funk, A.B. 1944; Mr. Funk, A.B. 1941; deceased November 16, 1976), and Kathryn Nell (Mrs. C. W. Compton, Jr., A.B. 1948).

Basketball began in 1902 at Indiana University, and Tommy, who had played on the first basketball team that Anderson High school had, played on the third basketball team in Indiana University's history during the 1902–1903 season.

He was elected Secretary of the Phi Kappa Psi social fraternity's alumni association in 1948; he had served previously as its national President (1932–34). He also served as Treasurer of the Indiana University Alumni Association from 1947 until he died on July 30, 1969.

Cookson was active in community affairs as well as University activities; he was a member of the Kiwanis and Masons and a deacon of the First Baptist Church of Bloomington.

He is buried in Valhalla Mausoleum.

Fenwick Thomas Reed, 1897–1980
Secretary, 1951–66

Fenwick Thomas Reed, administrator, son of Charles Fenwick and Helena (Fargher) Reed, was born July 15, 1897, in Terre Haute. He attended local schools through high school and then attended DePauw University from 1914 until he entered the United States Army (1917–19), where he obtained the rank of Lt. Colonel. He again returned to active service in World War II (1940–45).

Fen married Lucile Riley of Crawfordsville, Indiana, on November 20, 1920, and they had one son, James Fenwick (B.S. Purdue 1945).

After World War I, Reed became associated with Fletcher American National Bank of Indianapolis until 1930. During the next ten years (until 1940) he was associated with City Securities Corporation of Indianapolis and served as manager of the investments department of Newlin-Johnson Company of Terre Haute.

In 1940, he was ordered to active duty as the executive officer of the Indiana Military Area in Bloomington. The next year he was transferred to Indiana University as an ROTC instructor and served successively as battalion commander of

Fenwick Thomas Reed

the Army Specialized Training Program and as commandant of military personnel. He became assistant to then-President Herman B Wells (1945–51). Later, during Fen's tenure as a Secretary of the Trustees, he also functioned as the administration's chief liaison with the ROTC on the campus.

Reed became Secretary of the Board of Trustees 1951, succeeding Thomas A. Cookson who retired. Fen retired (1966) after twenty-five years of service to Indiana University. He was succeeded by Charles E. Harrell.

In addition to university duties, Fen was active in many civic affairs. Among those he served were the Indiana University division of the Bloomington Hospital Building Fund Drive (Chairman, 1961). He was Director of the Bloomington Hospital Board (Vice-President, 1964), on the Boards for the Monroe County Heart Association (1965), Monroe County United Fund Drive (manager, 1964), the YMCA, and the Selective Service Board.

Reed was a member of Sigma Nu social fraternity, the Elks, Reserve Officers Association, and the American Legion. He was a member of St. Marks Methodist Church and a Republican.

He died in 1980 and was buried at Valhalla Memory Gardens, Bloomington.

Charles Edwin Harrell, 1911–
Secretary, 1967–1981

Charles Edwin Harrell, administrator, son of Stacy Owen and Ada (Torrence) Harrell, was born January 16, 1911, in Bloomington, Indiana. He graduated from Bloomington High School and obtained an A.B. from Indiana University (1933). He attended Columbia University Law School (1933–34), but transferred back to Indiana University, obtaining the LL.B. (1936). This was supplemented by the J.D. (1967).

Charlie received letters in golf and as senior manager of the basketball team. He served as the University's golf coach (1954). During his college years he was a member of the

Charles Edwin Harrell

Board of Aeons (1932) and served out the uncompleted term of Leon Wallace as President (1933). He was a member of Sigma Chi social fraternity, a member of the Sphinx Club, an honorary social fraternity for upperclassmen, and of Phi Delta Phi, professional law fraternity.

Charlie, as he is best known, married Margaret Miriam Campbell on August 1, 1936, and they had a daughter, Jacqueline (Mrs. James Morris, B.S. 1965).

A month before commencement (1936) he started his first job at Indiana University as an assistant to Assistant Registrar Thomas A. Cookson, who, in addition to his own responsibilities, had been attempting to carry the work of the Registrar, who was ill. Charlie became Assistant Registrar (1940), Registrar (1948), and finally assumed the combined posts of Registrar and Director of Records and Admissions (1954). After more than thirty years in the Registrar's Office, Harrell became Secretary to the Board of Trustees (1967), which position he held until he retired (1981).

Charlie maintained an interest in campus affairs outside of his regular responsibilities and served as faculty advisor to Blue Key and to Dragons Head. His longest period of such service was to Sigma Chi. He was their Chapter Advisor for some twenty-eight years.

He holds membership in several professional organizations and is past president of the Indiana College Registrars Association and the American Association of Collegiate Registrars and Admissions Officers. He also is a member of the Indiana University Alumni Association, Bloomington Country Club, the Rotary, Masonic Lodge, Scottish Rite, Chamber of Commerce, and the Varsity Club. He served on the Board of the Community Chest, which pre-dated the United Fund, and on the Board of The United Fund with such service culminating in his being appointed General Chairman of the United Fund Drive in 1967.

During the annual summer retreat meeting of the Indiana University Board of Trustees (1980), Charlie was honored with the E. Ross Bartley Award in recognition of meritorious service.

After the University, Charlie's abiding love is still golf. He has won many trophies and has had the thrill of making a hole-in-one on four occasions. During a proposed trip to Europe he hopes to fulfill a long-time wish to play the St. Andrews course in Edinburgh, Scotland.

Harrell belongs to the United Methodist Church and is a Republican.

Robert Ermer Burton, 1918–
SECRETARY, 1981–

Robert E. Burton, educator and administrator, son of Loring Ermer and Edith (Roberts) Burton, was born in Kearney, Nebraska, on April 28, 1918. His parents were natives of Hamilton County, Indiana, and his father obtained an M.S. in Education from Indiana University (1940). In 1924 the family moved to Muncie, where his father taught school. Bob graduated from Burris High School in Muncie (1935) and then entered Ball State Teachers College (now Ball State University), where he obtained an A.B. in Education (1939).

Bob was active in a number of college activities. He was *"B" Book* Editor, Managing Editor and Summer Editor of *Ball State News*. He was a member of the YMCA (President, 1938–39); Pi Omega Pi, business education fraternity (President, 1938–39); Kappa Delta Pi, education fraternity (President, 1938–39); Alpha Phi Gamma, journalism fraternity; Blue Key, a service organization; and the Wesley Foundation (Methodist Church organization). He also worked at various jobs in the business office on a part-time basis (1935–40). He has taken some work toward a degree in Indiana University's School of Business (1952–57), and attended executive development workshops (1952 and 1953).

After graduating from Ball State, Bob taught commercial subjects at Bremen High School (1939–41).

On May 26, 1940, Bob married Mary Joan Smith of Westfield, Indiana, and they had five children: Ann E. (Mrs. Stephen J. Grimes; A.B. 1966, MAT 1971), John E. (B.S. 1968), Nancy E. (Mrs. Luis A. Morales, A.B. 1968), William L. (A.B., Earlham, 1971), and James E. Burton.

Robert Ermer Burton

Burton left teaching to become Assistant Cashier and Ticket Manager at Indiana University (1941–42), and then became Assistant to the Vice-President and Treasurer (1942–43). He was on military leave (September 1943 to January 1946), was discharged from HQ 15th Army as a Sergeant, and returned to his position at Indiana University. Bob later (1951–74) also assumed the responsibility of Assistant Secretary to the Board of Trustees. In July 1974 that position was changed to Assistant Secretary-Treasurer, Board of Trustees, and he served in this capacity until Charles E. Harrell retired as Secretary of the Board of Trustees in June 1981, at which time Burton became Secretary of the Board. However, he retained some of his responsibilities as Assistant to the Treasurer.

At IU Bob has been active in the Employees Credit Union (Board member, 1963–69; President, 1965–66); IU Retirement Community, Inc. (Assistant Treasurer, 1977–80; Board member and Treasurer, 1980–); Indiana Association of College and University Business Officers (President, 1959); Indiana-Purdue Foundation at Fort Wayne (Assistant Secretary, 1962–). He has served on numerous committees and has been a member of the IU Memorial Union Board of Directors (1969–72). In 1976 he was the recipient of the E. Ross Bartley Memorial Award.

Bob also has found time to be active in community affairs and long has been involved in the United Way (President, 1963; Board, 1960–65, 1977–1982, IU Campaign Chairman or Assistant Chairman, 1947–69; General Campaign Chairman 1977; Treasurer, 1978–1982), Kiwanis (member 1950–, president 1960, Lieutenant Governor, 1963), Kiwanis Indiana Foundation, Inc. (Board Member, Treasurer, 1973–), Kiwanis International Foundation (Life Fellow), Greater Bloomington Chamber of Commerce (Board, 1970–74; President, 1971–72; President's Advisory Committee, 1974–77). He is a Director of the Fountain Federal Savings and Loan Association (1957–) and holds memberships in the University Club, Riley Memorial Association, IU Alumni Association, Varsity Club, Friends of Music, IU Theatre Circle, School of Business Deans' Associates, Ball State Alumni Association, Society of Indiana Pioneers, Indiana Historical Society, Sons of American Revolution, National Audubon Society, Planned Parenthood Association, Monroe County Mental Health Association, and Stone Belt Council for Retarded Children.

Bob and his family enjoy camping and traveling. He and his wife have visited fifty states and more than thirty-five countries.· He also enjoys football and basketball, as well as classical music. He attends the First United Methodist Church (Trustee, 1973– , formerly was Chairman of the Official Board and Associate Lay Leader). He is a Republican.

John D. Mulholland, 1927–
Treasurer, 1974–

John D. Mulholland, educator and C.P.A., son of Harold Arnold and Jean Margaret (Dowsley) Mulholland, was born in Rochester, New York, on July 2, 1927.

He attended secondary school at Franklin Academy in Malone, New York. After serving in the U.S. Infantry, where most of his time was spent in the Army Band, he entered Clarkson College of Technology in Potsdam, New York, and obtained a B.B.A. (1950). He then went to the University of Michigan for an M.B.A. (1951). Jack, as he is better known, became a C.P.A. in New York State in 1958. Mulholland started his accounting career with Arthur Andersen and Company (1951–56) in New York City, moving to Dayton, Ohio, as assistant to the controller of H. C. Huber Construction Company, Inc. (1956–57). In 1957 he moved his family to Rochester, New York, where he was associated with General Dynamics (1957–61) as an internal auditor. An opportunity as Manager of General Accounting (1961–65) for Mead Johnson and Company brought the Mulhollands to Evansville, Indiana (1961–65). Jack advanced to Controller (1965–68); he also coordinated accounting and reporting matters during Mead and Johnson's merger with Bristol-Myers Company, having become Vice-President of Mead Johnsons' Operating Division (1968–69). He received the firm's President's Award in 1963.

He moved to Honolulu (1969) as Vice-President and Controller of Theo H. Davies and Company, Ltd., where he re-

John D. Mulholland

mained until he came to Indiana University (1972) as Assistant Vice-President for Financial Affairs. He was named Treasurer in 1974 and also acts as Treasurer for the Board of Trustees.

Jack married Patricia Walker on December 27, 1954, in Potsdam, New York, and they had three children: Gail Ellen (B.A. 1978), Joyce McLaren (Mrs. Sean St. Clair B.A. 1981, Mr. St. Clair B.S. 1981) and Wendy Walker (a junior in the Business School in 1982). Mrs. Mulholland has an M.S. (1977).

In college Jack was a member of Beta Alpha Psi (national accounting honorary fraternity, Sigma Delta social fraternity, accounting club, management club, Michigan Marching Band, Glee Club, was active in theatre plays, intramural sports and Ice Carnival affairs. He augmented his income from the G.I. education bill by playing in a dance band.

At Indiana University Jack has continued his interest in the theatre by his work with Indiana University's Theatre Circle, serving as President (1980–82). He also served as President of the University Club (1976–77). He is a member of the Central Association of College and University Business Officers (Executive Committee and he will become President in 1984). He has been a member of the American Institute of C.P.A.'s and the National Association of Accountants.

Mulholland also has been active in civic affairs. He was elected to a three-year term on the Board of Directors of the Greater Bloomington Chamber of Commerce (1979), and serves as their treasurer (1981–). He is a member of Big Brothers/Big Sisters of Monroe County, Treasurer of a high school booster club, active in the United Fund Allocations Committee and fund drive. He also was a Junior Achievement board member and past advisor. He attends the Methodist Church.

Jack teaches an advanced financial accounting course in the School of Business and also has taught accounting courses at Rochester Institute of Technology, evening division, and at the University of Hawaii.

Board of Trustees
Yearly Pictures

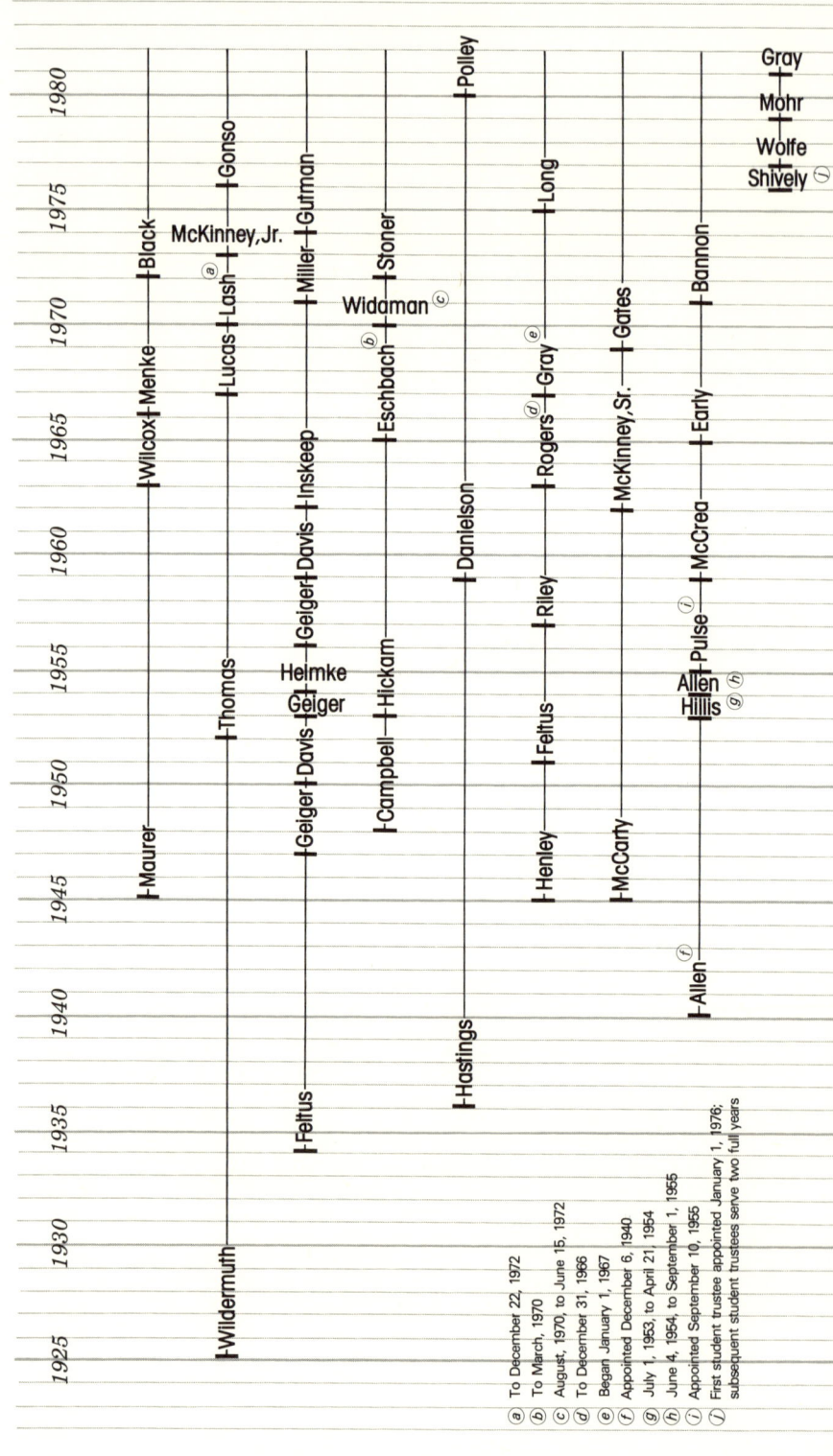

1949–50. From left to right around table: C. W. McCarty, A. M. Campbell, Mary Maurer, George Henley, Secretary Thomas Cookson, (standing), Ora Wildermuth, President Herman B Wells, Vice-President and Treasurer Joseph Franklin (standing), Dr. Dillon Geiger, John Hastings, Frank Allen, Vice-President Herman Briscoe.

1950–51. From left to right, top to bottom: Dr. Merrill Davis, George Henley, John Hastings, Ora Wildermuth, Mary Maurer, A. M. Campbell, Frank Allen, C. W. McCarty.

1951–52. From left to right around table: Ora Wildermuth, C. W. McCarty, Mary Maurer, John Hastings, Fenwick Reed (Trustee Secretary), Frank Allen, Dr. Merrill Davis, Paul Feltus.

1952–53. From left to right around table: Mary Maurer, C. W. McCarty, Ray C. Thomas, John Hastings, Fenwick Reed (Trustee Secretary), Paul Feltus, Frank Allen.

1953–54. From left to right around table: Fenwick Reed (Trustee Secretary), Dr. Dillon Geiger, Ray C. Thomas, Glen Hillis, John Hastings, Paul Feltus, Willis Hickham, Mary Maurer.

1954–55. From left to right around table: Walter Helmke, Ray C. Thomas, Frank Allen, Fenwick Reed (Trustee Secretary), John Hastings, C. W. McCarty, Paul Feltus (standing), Willis Hickham, Mary Maurer.

1955–56. From left to right around table: Walter Hemke, Ray C. Thomas, Earl Pulse, Fenwick Reed (Trustee Secretary), John Hastings, C. W. McCarty, Willis Hickham, Mary Maurer, Paul Feltus.

1956–57. From left to right around table: C. W. McCarty, Willis Hickham, Mary Maurer, Paul Feltus, John Hastings, Fenwick Reed (Trustee Secretary), Dr. Dillon Geiger, Ray Thomas, Earl Pulse.

1957–58. Standing, left to right: Ray Thomas, Willis Hickham, C. W. McCarty, Earl Pulse, Fenwick Reed (Trustee Secretary). *Seated, left to right:* John Hastings, Mary Maurer.

1958–59. From left to right around table: Fenwick Reed (Trustee Secretary), Willis Hickham, Mary Maurer, J. Stewart Riley, C. W. McCarty, John Hastings, George Henley (University Attorney), Dr. Dillon Geiger, Ray Thomas, Earl Pulse.

1959–60. From left to right around table: C. W. McCarty, J. Stewart Riley, Mary Maurer, Robert McCrea, Herman B Wells (President), Fenwick Reed (Trustee Secretary), Dr. Merrill Davis, Donald Danielson, Ray Thomas, Willis Hickham.

1960–61/1961–62. From left to right around table: Willis Hickham, J. Stewart Riley, Mary Maurer, Robert McCrea, Fenwick Reed (Trustee Secretary), Dr. Merrill Davis, Donald Danielson, Ray Thomas.

1962–63. From left to right around table: Fenwick Reed (Trustee Secretary), Harriett Inskeep, Donald Danielson, Ray Thomas, Willis Hickham, Frank McKinney, Sr., J. Stewart Riley, Mary Maurer, Robert McCrea.

1963–64. From left to right around table: Fenwick Reed (Trustee Secretary), Harriett Inskeep, Donald Danielson, Ray Thomas, Willis Hickham, Frank McKinney, Sr., Donald Rogers, Howard Wilcox, Robert McCrea.

1964–65. *From left to right:* Ray Thomas, Donald Rogers, Donald Danielson, Harriett Inskeep, Willis Hickham, Frank McKinney, Sr., Robert McCrea, Fenwick Reed (Trustee Secretary).

1965–66. *Seated:* Harriett Inskeep, Ray Thomas, Frank McKinney, Sr. *Standing:* Jesse Eschbach, Donald Danielson, Fenwick Reed (Trustee Secretary), John Early, Howard Wilcox, Donald Rogers.

1966–67. Seated: Harriett Inskeep, Frank McKinney, Sr., Ray Thomas. *Standing:* Donald Rogers, Jesse Eschbach, John Early, Donald Danielson, Robert Menke.

1967–68. From left to right around table: Charles Harrell (Trustee Secretary), Harriett Inskeep, Donald Danielson, Robert Lucas, Frank McKinney, Sr., Jesse Eschbach, Carl Gray, Robert Menke, John Early.

1968–69. From left to right around table: Vice-President Joseph Hartley, Harriett Inskeep, Donald Danielson, Robert Lucas, Frank McKinney, Sr., President Joseph Sutton, Jesse Eschbach, Carl Gray, Robert Menke, John Early, Vice-President Joseph Franklin.

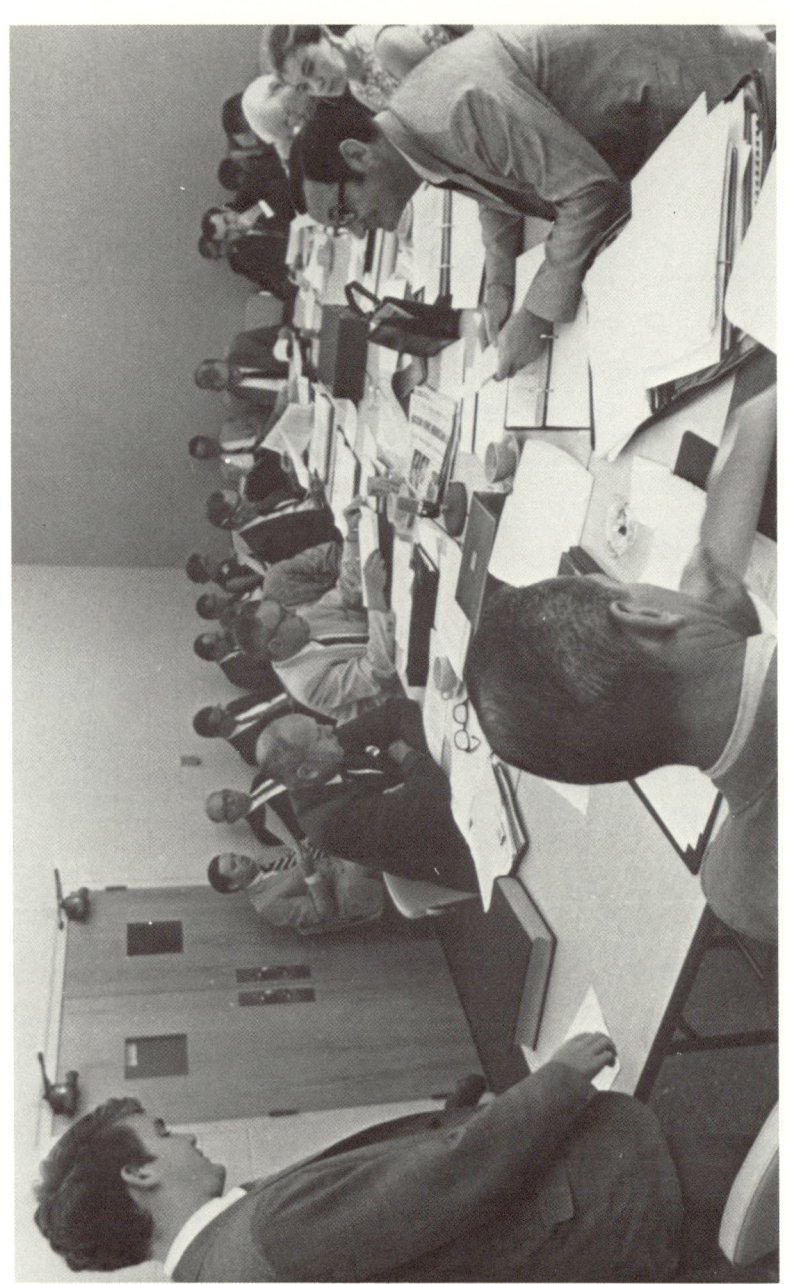

1969–70. Back to camera: Donald Danielson. Left to right around table: Paul Helmke (Student Body President), Robert Menke, Robert Gates, Vice-President Joseph Franklin, Vice-President David Derge, President Joseph Sutton, Carl Gray, Harriett Inskeep, Robert Lucas.

1970–71. Seated: Harriett Inskeep, Donald Danielson, John Widaman. *Standing:* Donald Lash, Robert Menke, Carl Gray, John Early, Robert Gates.

1971–72. *Seated*: Donald Danielson, Carl Gray, Jeanne Miller. *Standing*: Robert Gates, Dr. William Bannon, Robert Menke, John Widaman, Donald Lash, President John W. Ryan.

1972–73. Left to right: Donald Danielson, Carl Gray, Richard Stoner, Robert Gates, Dr. Joseph Balck.

1973–74. *From left to right around table:* Dr. William Bannon, Dr. Joseph Black, Jeanne Miller, Donald Danielson, Carl Gray, Robert Gates, Richard Stoner. *Standing, upper left:* Claude Rich, Vice-President W. George Pinnell, President John W. Ryan.

1974–75. Left to right around table: Dr. Joseph Black (back to photographer), Dr. William Bannon, Vice-President W. George Pinnell, Paul Klinge (assistant to the President), President John W. Ryan, Charles Harrell (Trustee Secretary), Carolyn Gutman, Carl Gray, Richard Stoner, Robert Gates, Donald Danielson, Howard Wilcox, Betty Hall (Secretary), Claude Rich, Chancellor Herman B Wells, Joseph Franklin, Vice-President Byrum Carter.

1975–76. Left to right: Donald Danielson, Clarence Long, Robert Gates, Dr. Joseph Black, Richard Stoner.

1976–77. *Back to camera, left to right:* Charles Harrell (Trustee Secretary), President John W. Ryan, Paul Klinge. *Left to right around table:* Carolyn Gutman, Leslie Shively (Student Trustee), Clarence Long, Robert Gates, Donald Danielson, Richard Stoner, Harry Gonzo, Dr. William Bannon, Dr. Joseph Black.

1977–78. *Left to right:* Carolyn Gutman, Betty Blumberg, Dr. Joseph Black, Dr. William Bannon, Richard Stoner, Robert Gates.

1978–79. Back to camera: Charles Harrell (Trustee Secretary), President John W. Ryan. *Left to right around table:* Betty Hall (Secretary), Carolyn Gutman, James Wolfe (Student Trustee), Clarence Long, Robert Gates, Donald Danielson, Harry Gonso, Dr. William Bannon, Dr. Joseph Black, Vice-President W. George Pinnell.

1979–80. *Front row, left to right:* Dr. William Bannon, John Stoner, Clarence Long, Donald Danielson, Dr. Joseph Black, William Mohr. *Second row:* President John W. Ryan, Harry Gonso, Carolyn Gutman, Charles Harrell (Trustee Secretary), Robert Gates.

1980–81. Front row, left to right: Dr. Joseph Black, William Mohr, Clarence Long, Harry Gonso, John Stoner. *Second row:* Robert Gates, Charles Harrell (Trustee Secretary), Carolyn Gutman, Dr. William Bannon, Betty Blumberg, President John W. Ryan, Vice-President W. George Pinnell.

1981–82. Seated, left to right: Richard Stoner (President), Harry Gonso, Clarence Long (Vice-President). Standing: Robert Gates, James Gray (Student Trustee), Carolyn Gutman, Dr. Joseph Black, Dr. William Bannon, Betty Blumberg Polley.

Index

Abrams, Janet E. Stoner 102
Acker, Kathleen Elynne Ryan 143
Acker, Kevin Ryan 143
Adams, Elizabeth G. 154
Adams, James S. 154
Allen, Frank Emerson 3–4, 269–72, 274
Anderson, Susan Jane Danielson 12
Anderson, Zetta Ann Franklin 179
Ashby, Marianna 189
Ashton, John William 159–61
Ashton, Richard 159
Austin, Virginia B. 102
Ayres, Catherine Alice Briscoe 168
Ayres, Stephen 168

Bannon, Jane Alexander 6
Bannon, William G., M.D. 4–7, 290, 292–93, 295–300
Barnhill, John R. 30
Batt, William L., Jr. 202
Bell, Mary Beatrice Ashton 159
Bell, Richard 159
Bellis, Beverly J. 193
Bennis, Warren 199
Berkfield, Dorothy Howland 127
Bernhardt, Mildred L. 61
Bernstein, Leonard 154
Berry, Katherine 77
Biddle, Ward G. 179, 255
Black, Beth 163
Black, Deborah Ann 7
Black, Joseph Morton, M.D. 7–9, 291–300
Bland, Congressman Oscar 23
Blumberg, Ben 88
Blumberg, Morris 88
Bogle, April 213
Bogle, Heather 213
Bogle, Victor Morton 212–14
Bonus, Thaddeus 161–63
Bowen, Margaret Merritt 194
Bowen, Governor Otis 27, 61, 87
Bowman, Sylvia Edmonia 214–17
Braden, David Black 163
Braden, John Black 163
Braden, Samuel Edward 163–66

Branigan, Governor Roger 21, 58, 99, 104, 130
Breimeyer, Alice Polley 88
Brennan, William J., Jr. (Supreme Court Justice) 199
Brilliant, Leanne Schwartz 245
Briscoe, Herman 167–69, 269
Briscoe, James Frederick 168
Briscoe, Robert Herman 168
Briscoe, William Cole 168
Brown, Harriett Kunkel 27
Broyles, Ralph Edward 217–19
Bryan, William Lowe 121
Burt, Pamela T. Stoner 102
Burton, James E. 261
Burton, John E. 261
Burton, William L. 261
Bush, Owen 74
Bussard, Aleta Lois 208

Campbell, Alexander Morton 9–12, 269–70
Campbell, Margaret Miriam 260
Campbell, Thomas Morton 11
Capehart, Senator Homer 11
Carmichael, Hoagy 154
Carrell, Janet Franklin 179
Carter, Byrum Earl, Jr. 169–71, 293
Carter, Keith Madison 171
Cassady, General E.B. 183
Church, Eleanor E. 11
Clark, Claire Marie McKinney 73
Clark, Cyrus J. 18
Clevenger, Lucile 23, 25
Cline, Ruth Adele 188
Cole, Orah 168
Collins, David Harrington 173
Collins, Ralph Leonard 172–74
Compton, Kathryn Nell Cookson 255
Cookson, Ruth Eliza 255
Cookson, Thomas Aubrey 255–56, 258, 260, 269
Costello, Edward J. 159
Costello, Elizabeth Ashton 159
Craig, Dorothy Ellen 173
Craig, Governor George N. 3, 27, 50
Cravens, John William 255

301

Crawford, Lynn Ellen Bannon 6
Crooks, Alice 221
Crooks, Ann 221
Crooks, Edwin William 220–22

Daly, Debra Lynn Liebenow 193
Danielson, Donald Carroll 12–15, 104, 279–95, 297–98
Davis, Joseph 18
Davis, Merrill Stamper, M.D. 15–18, 270–71, 279, 280
Davis, Richard 17
DeMarcus, Mary Josephine 17
Denning, Pamela Bannon 6
Derge, David Richard, Jr. 174–77, 288
Derge, David Richard III 174
Derge, Dorothy Anne 174
Derge, Mary Jennifer 174
Derge, William David 174
Douglas, Senator Paul 202
Dudley, Sarah Alice 228
Dykes, Helen Allen 3

Early, John Ehret 18–20, 284–87, 289
Edwards, Susan Annette Black 7
Eisenhower, President Dwight D. 43, 83, 129
Elliott, Ruth 51
Elsner, Edward Peter 7
Elsner, Mary A. 7
Elson, Karen 199
Eschbach, Jesse E. II 21–23, 108, 284, 285, 286, 287
Eschbach, Jesse E. III 21
Evans, Esther 250
Evens, Alfred 69

Feltus, Paul Lambert 23–26, 30, 271–74
Fickel, Elba 50
Foulke, Harriett 231
Franklin, Joseph Amos 177–80, 201, 269, 287–88, 293
Franklin, Joseph Arnold 179
Franklin, Richard Paul 179
Funk, Clara Louise Cookson 255
Funk, J. Hugh 255

Gates, Benton E. 27
Gates, Mary Ellen 27
Gates, Robert Edwards 26–28, 288–300
Gavit, Bernard Campbell 51
Geiger, Dillon Donald, M.D. 18, 28–31, 269, 273, 276, 278
Giusti, Joseph Paul 222–25
Giusti, Lynn Christine 224
Giusti, Susan Marie 224

Goerke, Glenn Allan 225–28
Goerke, Jill A. 227
Goerke, Kurt E. 227
Goerke, Lynn E. 227
Gonso, Christopher Lee 31
Gonso, Harry Lee 31, 295, 297–300
Gonso, Helen Irene 31
Gonso, Matthew Henry 31
Good, Elizabeth Walker Early 20
Gooday, D. Patricia 143
Graham, Dorothy E. 201
Gray, B. Diane Liebenow 193
Gray, Carl M. 33–36, 286–93
Gray, James Walter 36–38, 300
Gray, Virginia 36
Greene, Elizabeth Anne 174
Greene, J. E. 174
Griffin, Marjorie G. Gates 27
Grigsby, Joyce 207
Grigsby, Melborn 207
Grigsby, Mildred Sutton 207
Grimes, Ann E. Burton 261
Grizzell, Jane G. Hickam 51
Grohsmeyer, Erik Andrew 228
Grohsmeyer, Frederick Andrew 228
Grohsmeyer, Frederick Andrew, Jr. 228–30
Gros Louis, Amy Catherine 180
Gros Louis, Julie Jeannette 180
Gros Louis, Kenneth R. R. 180–83
Gucker, Frank T. 152
Gutman, Carolyn Prickett 38–40, 293, 295–300
Gutman, Gretchen Kay 38
Gutman, Kurt Alan 38
Gutman, Phillip Edward 38
Gutman, Phillip Edward, Jr. 38

Hamilton, Alexander 23
Hamilton, Natalie Henley 50
Hammond, Jean Talbott Wright 208
Harkness, Jean 137
Harrell, Charles Edwin 258–61, 263, 293, 295, 297–99
Harris, Honore 66
Hart, Paula Lucile Clevenger 23
Hartley, Greg 183
Hartley, Joseph Robert 183–86, 287
Hartley, Karen Louise 183
Hartley, Lynn Marie 183
Haskell, Rachel Blumberg 88
Hastings, Howell 41
Hastings, James Roland 43
Hastings, John Simpson 41–44, 269–78
Hastings, Joshua 41
Hastings, Joshua, Jr. 41

Index

Hastings, William Elmer 43
Haynes, Bernice 55
Haynes, Elwood 55
Hedrick, Terry Elizabeth Carter 169
Heetderks, Bernard, M.D. 203
Heetderks, Katherine Corlett 203
Heetderks, Margaret Ann 203
Heffner, Christopher 188
Heffner, David 188
Heffner, Ray Lorenzo, Jr. 186–89
Heidenreich, Marjorie 108
Helmke, W. Paul 44, 288
Helmke, Walter Edward 44–47, 270, 275
Helmke, Walter P. 44
Henderson, Judith Ann Early 20
Henley, George Washington 47–50, 269–70, 278
Henley, Henry 47, 49
Henley, Joseph 49
Henley, Martha 47
Henley, Patrick 47
Hickam, Elliott 51
Hickam, Lt. Col. Horace M. 53
Hickam, Hubert 53
Hickam, Willis 51–53, 273–83
Hillis, Elwood 55
Hillis, Glen Raymond 3, 53–56, 273
Hillis, Joseph 55
Hillis, Margaret 55
Hillis, Robert 55
Hine, Maynard Kiplinger 231–34
Hine, Maynard Kiplinger, Jr. 231
Hine, William Clyde 231
Hinkle, Thelma 25
Hoffman, Theresa Blumberg 88
Hogue, Virginia B. 240
Houseworth, Barbara Marie Rogers 99
Houseworth, John H. 99
Hovde, Frederick L. 130
Huber, Florence Elizabeth 159, 160
Hyde, Judith Hine 231

Inskeep, Harriett Simmons 13, 56–59, 281–84
Inskeep, Joseph Glenn 58
Inskeep, Richard Glenn 58
Inskeep, Stephen Simmons 58
Inskeep, Thomas Richard 58
Irwin, Glenn Ward, Jr., M.D. 189–91
Irwin, William 189

Johnson, President Lyndon B. 138
Johnson, Sheila McCarty 66
Josephson, Elizabeth 138
Judson, Margaret Anne Grohsmeyer 228

Karlson, Dagmar 95
Kelly, Josephine 105
Kennedy, President John F. 202
Kirts, Rebecca Lee Stoner 102
Klinge, Paul 293, 295
Knipe, Morna Hickam 53
Knight, Robert "Bobby" 150
Koors, Krista Widaman 108
Kuhn, Kathryn Widaman 108
Kunkel, William 12

Laird, Byron F. 221
Lash, David Roy 59
Lash, Donald Ray 32, 289–90
Lash, Marguerite Sue 59
Lash, Russell Earl 59
Latham, Sue Bannon 6
Lauritzen, Jonni 31
Liebenow, J. Gus 191–94
Liebenow, Jay Stanton 193
Liebenow, John Stuart 193
Lindley, Jonathan 47
Lindley, Mary Ann 47
Lloyd, Russell G. 102
Logan, Louise Evelyn 183
London, Mae R. 115
Long, Beatrice 179
Long, Bruce Allen 61
Long, Clarence William 61–63, 294–95, 297–300
Long, David John 61
Long, William Randall 61
Lowe, Joyce Dunford 110
Lucas, Robert Anthony 63–66, 286, 287, 288
Lyons, R. E. 166

MacArthur, General Douglas III 137
McCarty, Charles Walter 66–68, 269–72, 274–79
McCoy, Mary Ann Polley 88
McCray, Mary Ann Pulse 91
McCrea, David Smith 69
McCrea, Edward Franklin 69
McCrea, Elizabeth Statts 69
McCrea, Robert Franklin 67–71, 279–83
McCrea, Thomas 69
McDonald, Mae 7
McKinney, Ann Kathleen 71
McKinney, Frank Edward, Jr. 73
McKinney, Frank Edward, Sr. 71–75, 281–87
McKinney, Frank E. III 77
McKinney, George 71
McKinney, Heather Claire 77
McKinney, Katherine Marie 71, 77

McKinney, Lydia 71
McKinney, Madeleine Warner 77
McKinney, Margaret Leonard 77
McKinney, Robert Warner 73, 77
Macmillan, Prime Minister (Maurice) Harold 50
McMurtie, Phyllis 82
McNeill, Robert Joseph 234-37
Mahigian Smith, Cynthia Ellen Williams 207
Marler, Linda Merritt 196
Mathers, William Hammond 154
Maurer, Mary Rieman 78-80, 269-81
Maurer, William F. 80
Mazza, Marie D. 224
Mendenhall, Margaret 59
Menke, David 82
Menke, Robert Henry 80-83, 285-90
Menke, Robert, Jr. 82
Merritt, Lynn R. 196
Merritt, Lynne Lionel, Jr. 194-97
Meyerson, Martin 199
Michael, Rachel 63
Middendorf, Karen Menke 82
Miller, Carl Michael 85
Miller, Jeanne Seidel 83-85, 290, 292
Miller, Marjorie A. 85
Miller, Mickey M. 85
Miller, Ward W. 85
Mitchum, Louise 30
Moffat, Georgabell Henley 50
Mohr, William Hall 85-87, 298-99
Montague, Wallace 208
Montgomery, Field Marshall Bernard Law 110
Moore, Kathleen Allen 3
Morales, Nancy E. Burton 261
Morris, Jacqueline Harrell 260
Moss, Jacobena 71
Moss, Philip 71
Mulholland, Gail Ellen 266
Mulholland, John D. 264-66
Mulholland, Wendy Walker 266
Myers, Eulala 33, 36

Nixon, President Richard M. 176
Nolan, Val F. 4

O'Neil, Benjamin 199
O'Neil, David 199
O'Neil, Elizabeth 199
O'Neil, Peter 199
O'Neil, Robert M. 197-99
Orescanin, Danilo 237-40
Orescanin, Danilo II 237
Orescanin, Lori 237
Orr, Governor Robert 28

Penrod, Bruce 240
Penrod, Caroline 240
Penrod, Kenneth Earl 240-42
Petach, Elizabeth Anne Wright 208
Peter, Beth 169
Peters, Norman K. 21
Peters, Virginia Eschbach 21
Peterson, Patricia Jane 12
Pinnell, William George 200-203, 292-93, 297, 299
Polak, Mildred Z. 115
Pollard, Lourdes C. 102
Polley, Elizabeth Blumberg 88-91, 196, 299-300
Polley, Howard F. 88
Polley, William 88
Pulse, Earl Burton 6, 91-93, 275-78
Pulse, Earl B., Jr. 91
Pyle, Ernie 107

Quayle, Senator Dan 118

Rawles, W.A. 121
Redman, Anne E. Gates 27
Reed, Fenwick Thomas 256-58, 271-73, 275-84
Reed, James Fenwick 256
Rich, Claude T. 292, 293
Riley, John Stewart 93-97, 278-81
Riley, Katherine Anne 95
Riley, Lucile 256
Rogers, Donald A. 35, 97-100, 282-85
Rogers, John William 99
Rogers, Leon B. 100
Rogers, Leon David 99
Rogers, Marion C. 97
Rogers, Virginia 97
Ryan, John William 140, 142-55, 290, 292, 293, 295, 297-98
Ryan, Kerrick Charles Casey 143
Ryan, Kevin Dennis Mitchell 143.

St. Clair, Joyce McLaren Mulholland 266
St. Clair, Sean 266
Schatzlein, Mary Carroll Danielson 12
Scheele, Mary Ann Helmke 44
Schenk, Fern Jewell 213
Schiffli, Elizabeth Irwin 189
Schilt, Alexander F. 243-45
Schilt, Kristen Rose 243
Schilt, Paige Eileen 243
Schleuniger, Joan 221
Schricker, Governor Henry F. 18
Schwartz, Bradley F. 245
Schwartz, Donald 245-47
Schwartz, Lois 245

Schwartz, Mark W. 245
Schwartz, Scott B. 245
Seashore, Stanley E. 237
Shively, Leslie Curtis 100-102, 295
Shoemaker, Raymond L. 152
Simmons, Hazel 91
Smiley, Mary Esther 41
Smith, Dorothy Ruth 69
Smith, Mary Joan 261
Smith, Patricia 249
Snyder, Charlotte 243
Snyder, Kathryn Dee 203
Snyder, John William 203-205
Snyder, Mark Alan 203
Stahr, Bradford Lanier 127
Stahr, Elvis Jacob, Jr. 127-35
Stahr, Stephanie Ann 127
Stahr, Stuart Edward Winston 127
Stoltz, Carolyn Louise Helmke 44
Stoner, Benjamin A. 102
Stoner, Joanne J. 102
Stoner, Richard B. 102-104, 291-96, 298-300
Stoner, Richard B., Jr. 102
Stowe, Georgia Graham Pinnell 201
Sutton, Abigail 137
Sutton, David 137
Sutton, Elmer 137
Sutton, James 137
Sutton, Jeffrey 137
Sutton, Joseph Lee 123, 137-41, 144, 147, 176, 287, 288
Sutton, Wilber 137
Swaim, H. Nathan (Judge) 63

Tatelman, Gretchen Blumberg 88
Taylor, Barbara Ellen McCrea 69
Taylor, Jay Gordon 69
Thomas, Joseph 105
Thomas, Ray Cecil 105-107, 272-85
Thompson, Amy Elizabeth Danielson 12
Thompson, Cheri 249
Thompson, Hugh Lee 247-50
Thompson, Jane L. 7
Thompson, Linda 249
Thompson, Tempe 249
Thompson, Vicki 249
Truman, President Harry S 11
Tuck, Betty 110
Tula, Maxine Wildermuth 115

Van Nuys, John 18

Walda, Julia Ann Inskeep 58
Walker, Ann G. 20
Walker, Joyce Leslie 227
Walker, Patricia 266
Walker, Sara A. 21
Wallace, Leon 260
Walstrum, Martha Virginia Clevenger 23
Warden, Ann Irwin 189
Warner, Frank 71
Warner, Katherine 71
Warner, Margaret K. 71
Wehrenberg, Wilma L. 44
Weimer, Arthur 168, 201
Weir, Reid 82
Weir, Susan Menke 82
Wells, Herman B 31, 121-23, 138-39, 269, 279, 293
Welsh, Governor Matthew E. 58, 201
West, Mary Beth Braden 163
Whitcomb, Governor Edgar D. 27, 43, 53
White, Mignon 255
Widaman, John Daniel II 108-109, 289-90
Widaman, John D. III 108
Widaman, Karen 108
Widman, Lucille Elizabeth 194
Widman, O. W. 194
Wilcox, David Warren 110
Wilcox, Donald DuVall 110
Wilcox, Howard Samuel 110-13, 282, 284, 293
Wilcox, Howard S., Jr. 110
Wilcox, Scott Robert 110
Wildermuth, Ora Leonard 57, 107, 113-16, 269-71
Wilds, Cordelia 115
Williams, Catherine E. 217
Williams, Edgar Gene 205-208
Williams, Lucille Merritt 194
Williams, N. N. 217
Williams, Patricia Jean 174
Williams, Thomas Gene 207
Winandy, Dolores 180
Wolfe, James Willard 116-18, 297
Wolfe, Kathleen Virginia 237
Wolfe, William (Bill) 116
Wolfson, Alice Jeannette 250
Wolfson, George Stephen 250
Wolfson, Lester Marvin 250-52
Wolfson, Margaret Gail 250
Woolery, Laura Marie 99
Wright, Wendell William 208-10

Young, Evelyn Regina 236